Sage Advice
Concerning Paranormal Events

Claudia Williams

LEFT HAND PRESS
A subsidiary of Black Moon Publishing LLC
CINCINNATI, OHIO
USA

Black Moon Manifesto

It is the Will and mission of Bate Cabal/Black Moon to effectively manifest unique and insightful occult Works for the esoteric community in a manner that is unfettered by commercial considerations.

Copyright © 2021 Claudia Williams
All rights reserved.

Design © 2021 Black Moon Publishing,LLC

Published by Left Hand Press
a subsidiary of Black Moon Publishing,LLC

BlackMoonPublishing.com

blackmoonpublishing@gmail.com

Design and layout by
Jo Bounds of Black Moon

ISBN: 978-1-890399-90-0

United States • United Kingdom • Europe • Brazil • Australia • India • Japan

CONTENTS

Introduction 5
   A Little About Me 8

Haunting Types 13
   Residual or Place Memeory Haunting 13
   Active Hauntings 15
   Interactive Hauntings 16
   Can a Person or Item Be Haunted? 33
   Ghosts 55
   What the Hell Was That Thing? 58
   Doppelgangers 61
   Poltergeists 63
   Demons 67
   Something Unusual is Going On - How Do I Handle It? . . . 82
   Money 85
   How Do I Properly Spiritually Cleanse My Things/Place? . . 86
   A Few Words About Salt 95
   Smudging 97
   Salt/Holy Water Blessing 99
   Candles 100

Conclusion 101

Introduction

By most written accounts, it is probably fair to say hauntings and supernatural activity of one sort or another have plagued or blessed (depending on your perception and the situation) us since we began finding ways to record history. From the earliest cave drawings found in areas all over the world depicting what appear to be negative spirits to cases written about in recognized language over the last 500 years, living humans, it seems have been dealing with problems in their environments (homes, workplaces, outside areas in which they must work or through which they must travel) for many centuries if not longer.

Recently, a new aeon approach to "finding the truth" about such events has led millions of people to a new awareness/acknowledgement that something really is out there. This is good. That same hunger for categorizing and "fixing," "healing" or "cleansing" the problems, while generally well meaning, may be problematic. This can be useless endeavor at best and woefully ill advised in the worst situations. My intention with this book is to help people understand and identify what may or may not be going on in their space and then know what the best approach is to handling the situation. It is my firm belief that talking about these issues and each of us sharing our experiences just unto itself is healing and can take away much of the terror of feeling alone dealing with such a situation. That alone is huge. The more

people learn and the more people realize they are not the only ones to have some paranormal event touch their lives, the better. It is not my intention that this be a "How To" book for potential ghost hunters. Nevertheless, I will be talking about tools used by paranormal Investigators – what they do, why they are useful. I will not endeavor to teach the reader how an item is used simply because different manufacturers of the same basic equipment will make their items slightly differently. If you are interested in ghost hunting, when you get your equipment, read the instructions!

The truth is there is very little absolutely agreed upon as fact where science is concerned regarding the paranormal. As much study, investigation and, in some cases, interaction as some of us do and have with these energies, most of what we know or believe we know still counts as theory and nothing absolute. Nevertheless, the numbers of cases continue to rise. The number of people who have dealt with "something" whether they have an exact term for it or not gets greater all the time. In many cases, no doubt this is simply due to the fact that as more people talk about it happening to them, others feel more comfortable coming forward with their stories. This is a good thing. In pretty much every area of human psychology and the human psyche virtually every professional in fields involving these matters will say that keeping dark, difficult secrets is an agreed upon formula for personal emotional and even physical disaster. Releasing the stories of these fears and experiences seems to help disempower them almost immediately.

It is not my interest here to argue the existence of the paranormal. I have no interest in that. I have seen, heard and worked with too many situations that should not have been able to happen to have

any interest in being told they really did not. I have worked with too many other people whose experience have been too similar (it's not just me). I also believe there is ample scientific evidence through all sorts of documentation; interviews with witnesses, documented consistent changes in atmospheric conditions where none should occur, recorded voice/sound phenomena, video recordings to name a few - to any longer argue the existence of what we presently term "paranormal" activity. I have no interest in arguing the existence of the Supernatural. While admittedly, the study of the myriad of subjects that fall under this wide umbrella term are largely in their infancy, I believe ample evidence exists to demonstrate that in the case of spirit/ghost even demonic activity SOMETHING REAL exists. No, I freely admit we do not have all the answers, but real things go on and effect all kinds of people in very real and sometimes life altering ways. I feel there is no discounting this. I direct the information here to the people who have come to believe as I do and want or perhaps due to experiences they are encountering, need to learn more. I particularly write this book for those who have learned burning mass amounts of sage, white sage, clary sage, sage with lavender, sage with cedar, sage of any kind combined with any number of other things - is not always the answer. It may not do anything at all, let alone make all one's metaphysical problems go away. On occasion it can do more harm than good. This book is for the people who have a deeper interest or need to understand what steps and actions can be taken under what particular circumstances to gain some kind of control over unseen forces they may be battling.

My purpose here is to explain certain concepts and theories

about ghosts and the paranormal and help educate the curious as well as hopefully empower those who believe they may be experiencing some kind of phenomenon.

As I have already stated, this is not intended to be an instructional book for the would be ghost hunter. Primarily because ghost hunting is a little different for everyone, can be an expensive endeavor and, honestly, it can be a dangerous one. That said, later on I will give some basic advice and general rules for those whose personal situations may be necessitating they become more savvy about verification of paranormal activity, living with it or removing it.

A Little About Me

I have been a psychic and medium my whole life. I became fascinated with hauntings and paranormal/supernatural activity when I was a child in New York City and on a school trip we visited the historic and notorious Morris-Jumel Mansion in Upper Manhattan. The tour guides gleefully told the ghost stories about the house to our audience of eight year olds. While we experienced nothing direct or obvious at that time, I knew there was something about that house. There was at least one person (it felt to me like more) living there and watching as their stories were told. I felt sorry for some, dubious of others. I sensed the stories as they were being told and as the spirits who lived them had perceived them in life did not jibe. The house obsessed me. I would go over and over the tales of the ghosts looking for answers.

All of my teachers were aware of how taken I had been with

the house, the Revolutionary and Civil War (the Jumel Mansion played a role in each) and the ghost stories. About a year later, when I was nine I went to one of my teachers with a disturbing dream I had had the night before. There had been a mannequin in the house dressed as the lady of the house, Mrs. Jumel, who had been accused of killing her husband by ripping off his bandages after a serious accident and leaving him to bleed to death in their bedroom. In my dream, I had seen the mannequin. It was calling to me. And as it did, it stood waist high in fire. About a day or two later I recall being called out of class into the hallway of the school. At that time there was a collection of Upper West Side townhouses which had been connected to make one maze-like building. (The Calhoun School is very much still in existence, but has since been torn down and replaced by a Godforsaken modern structure resembling a television or microwave oven depending on one's aesthetic). The teacher I had spoken with and another administrative assistant had peculiar and disturbed looks on their faces. I imagine in order to thwart some strange nine year old histrionics, they had taken me out of class to tell me privately "some very disturbing news" they didn't want me to hear elsewhere. The night before some people had tried to burn down the Morris-Jumel Mansion. It had received some serious damage. They each looked down at me as waiting for my seizure to start. I remember saying, "I'm very sorry to hear that. That's terrible." I did not approve of vandalism. Evidently, there were rumors the arsonists had been area people who had become familiar with the ghost stories and in fear (and ignorance) decided to end the evil by destroying the building. I recall thinking to myself, "So THAT'S

~ 9

what Mrs. Jumel was trying to tell me." I looked at the lovely Miss Hicks, my teacher, and the administrative person and asked if we could go back to class. They both seemed perplexed by my attitude. It wasn't the first time, it wouldn't be the last, I knew, that information would come to me about events upcoming or events that had taken place and were misunderstood. My greatest question was why I had received the information when given my age especially as well as other circumstances, there was nothing I could have done to stop it. My connection to that house and its reach would remain.

In 2005 after Hurricane Katrina my husband and I had to temporarily relocate back to New York, mandatory evacuation was in effect. While there one day I made the pilgrimage to the Uptown cemetery where my father's ashes are interred. A good Vodoun, I took him a little bottle of his favorite gin, favorite smokes and a rose. I needed to use discretion as, religious purposes or not, this cemetery has made it clear they frown on anything other than flowers left near a grave and my booze and cigarette offering would be nothing but garbage to their grounds people. It was a chilly overcast New York City Fall day. I talked to my father for a while, explained where I lived now and what I was doing, though I had no doubt he already knew. When finally I turned around to face the hill of old crypts my dad's drawer faces I was startled to see that directly across from him was an old aboveground crypt such as we have in New Orleans. The name over the iron door read clearly, "Jumel." How I had never noticed this before I have no idea. I climbed across the driveway and up to it to pay my respects. As expected, I could see the crypt

was closed, but I thought I would offer a prayer. Upon reaching it, I was startled to see the heavy iron door open by itself as if inviting me inside. There was a chill in the air and the skies were grey, but there was no wind. Particularly not one strong enough to move this kind of door. I hesitated for a moment, but entered. In fact, the crypt was entirely empty. I talked to it a bit anyway as something had obviously wanted my attention. I even closed the door and requested that whoever opened it for me the first time do so again. This time I would video anything that happened with my new Katrina replacement Motorola cell phone. Upon request, the door did open again. I kept that video for almost two years and showed it to many people before the phone was lost. A serious regret as I hadn't been able to send it elsewhere to save it. Cell phone pictures and video in 2005 were much less advanced than they are today. I have no doubt I will somehow connect to the house and its former inhabitants again when the time is right.

I have lived in a home in New Orleans for 25 years which is and has been for many years very active paranormally. Enough so, in fact, that we hold investigations up to five nights a week during which we teach people about the tools of investigating unexplained activity as well as how to debunk certain common things often experienced but, which really are generated from the most mundane sources. I am a professional psychic medium, a professional occultist and Priestess in New Orleans Vodou. My husband and I own the oldest Occult shop in New Orleans, Starling Magickal Occult Shop. I also belong to a paranormal activity investigation team, Darklight Paranormal, New Orleans. Here, I have the privilege of working with two of

the best and most dedicated Investigators I have ever met, Rob Pryor, our technology specialist and Michael Bill also known as #MichaelBillGhostHunter who is one of the people most knowledgeable about paranormal activity in all its forms I have ever come across. We have a great team. I bring the psychic medium skills to the group. We all can use the various devices for identifying unusual energy or communicating with spirits. We teach people in my house, but we consult on cases and investigate other places as well. Michael and I have a greater background in religious and occult theory, while Rob has a vast knowledge of the latest and greatest technology for measuring the slightest disturbances in an atmosphere. A good paranormal investigative team needs to be knowledgeable and needs to have an extreme level of trust between each other. We are blessed to have both.

Haunting Types

As a rule, it is generally agreed among paranormal researchers and investigators there are three kinds of haunting phenomena connected to places.

Residual or Place Memory Haunting

In my estimation, this is by far the most common form of paranormal activity. It is exactly as it sounds. This kind of haunting works on the theory that various places, buildings, etc. have the capacity to somehow "record" events which took place there in the past. This is especially true for situations in which a particular sound, movement, event took place again and again over a specific period of time. Usually, years.

Examples of this are empty prisons where visitors still hear the sounds of cell doors opening and closing long after the place itself has ceased to function as a working prison. In my book, "Haunted Spaces, Public Places" (originally published by Starling Books, 2004) I wrote about one of my favorite examples of this. In the French Quarter of New Orleans on Chartres Street what is now the Williams Research Center housed for many years the area police department. To this day, at night especially, people see police car lights flashing their reflection in the windows. Some people never think about it and simply assume a police car with its lights on is passing. For those who do have reason to turn

~ 13

their heads, they're often startled to discover there is no police car with lights going by. When the building was a police precinct, the officers would frequently get quickly out of the vehicles while leaving the lights running to bring in someone they'd arrested or do some quick task. This went on day and night for decades. It is easy to imagine that somehow the windows still see those lights, even if they are no longer stopping there.

Personally, I am convinced my heirs will hear the sound of pop tops opening for all the thousands of cans of Diet Dr. Pepper I have opened in the house over the years.

So, you get the point. Residual hauntings can be sights, sounds, scents, things of that nature. This includes voices or images of people moving around. While they can be startling, they are harmless. They are recordings in the air or walls of a place with no consciousness or awareness at all. One theory holds that in some cases the very walls of buildings are comprised of the same materials that make up magnetic recording tape. The belief is that somehow the walls have literally managed to record sounds once heard constantly only to somehow play them back and continue to play them back years and years after. I personally theorize this might be particularly easy if a structure made of these elements was, for example, hit by lightning while the sound was going on. Could the electric shock embed the sound as a recording device does on tape? This is simply my own theory and there are many. There may actually be many ways this happens. We don't know this part yet. We do know what we call residual or place memory hauntings are not much more than a nuisance and unfortunately, in general there is little that can be done to stop them. Most

people who find themselves in a home or building with a Residual Haunting come to realize it is harmless and learn to live with it.

Active Hauntings

This is the area where paranormal activity starts to get trickier to identify and deal with. With an Active Haunting, there is physical activity that takes place. By this I mean papers moving around, tapping sounds in walls or coming from unidentifiable spots. Lights and electronics may turn on and off by themselves. Doors may open and close on their own.

When I say these are more difficult to identify I mean it is generally agreed that this kind of activity can be indicative of both Place Memory or Interactive Hauntings which we will discuss next.

Sometimes things can move about as the result of electromagnetic anomalies that can be measured, but do not appear to be associated with any intelligent instigator. That would certainly explain things like televisions turning on and off by themselves or lights or other electrical devices. It is possible that knocking sounds can be the result of recorded sounds embedded in the atmosphere of a place. However, when items like keys or shoes start being moved or "A-Ported" it is difficult to find a reason for this that falls into the category of Place Memory or Active Haunting without there being a consciousness behind it. These are things that seem geared to garner attention from the person whose papers, keys or other personal items are going missing only to often be found elsewhere in the space in some bizarre spot

they were not and would never have been placed by the owner. Thus, determining whether activity is Active or Interactive can be difficult at times. In general, an Active Haunting is one in which there are sounds or scents or there are apparitions, but there is no demonstration by the phenomena that there is any awareness of the people witnessing them. These can be extremely upsetting, but are generally not dangerous.

Interactive Hauntings

In the world of paranormal investigation Interactive Hauntings are something of a holy grail to find and try and learn about. Simply put, an Interactive Haunting is one in which there is an energy (or possibly more than one energy/entity) which clearly is aware of the presence of the living people in the home or building and makes identifiable efforts to communicate. The most common forms of communication include voices that can be heard clearly without the assistance of any devices. On the other hand, EVPs or Electronic Voice Phenomena can also be picked by recording devices, both ones designed specifically to be more sensitive to such sound, but sometimes by regular recording devices as well. In these cases a question is generally asked, some time given for a response (we tend to give about 15 to 20 seconds) and then the question and possible response played back. Much of the time there is no response as much of paranormal investigation, even in places where activity has been documented, is sitting and waiting. There are those extraordinary times though, when a response is

received and gives a direct answer to a question. Often an entity will give its name, an explanation as to why it is in the space and other information. One of my favorite examples of this though was an EVP session we held in my own Interactively haunted home where a question was asked about a possible future event. The spirit's response was, "I don't know. I am dead, not psychic." We know the spirits in our home and while this answer may sound somewhat disturbing, it was actually said with a bit of humor. However, for the person who asked and those in attendance, it was enlightening. Just because spirits are on the other side, why should they be expected to know the future?

With an active paranormal energy, one can put out an object such as a flash light or light with special sensors designed for the purpose and place it at least 8 or 10 feet from where any human could have contact with it and then talk to a ghost and ask it if it is in the room with us at the time, will it please turn on the flashlight or pass by the sensor light. It never ceases to amaze me when they do comply and turn the lights on and off in answer to various questions. It is one way of having a real time conversation with a spirit. Sometimes, they like to use their own ways. We have one spirit who enjoys flushing the toilet in order to answer questions. We periodically have to remind this one that the cost of water and sewer bills in the French Quarter is especially high and we really appreciate it if they use one of the other devices we offer to get a message through.

As I said earlier, on occasion, spirits will speak loudly enough that they can be heard with the naked ear. That is truly an extraordinary experience. There are also a plethora of electronics

with the ability to give ghosts a way to speak in words an answer questions. The Ovulis which has a word bank of thousands of words and theoretically takes the energy its picking up and translates it into the appropriate word the entity is trying to say. Then there are the SB-7 or SB-11 boxes (with newer and more advanced versions coming all the time) which sweep through radio frequencies at the rate of dozens or more a second. The theory here is that it would be impossible to pick up a single radio station signal radio station signal long enough for a full sentence to be heard, let alone a full sentence that directly and usefully answers a question asked of a spirit. These devices work quite well for getting verbal information. Their only drawbacks are the sounds of the radio frequencies being swept can be very loud and annoying and these are battery operated items. In theory, other worldly energies can gain strength by absorbing electronic energy. This seems to be easier done via batteries than by using household appliances plugged into a wall and running on current. There are some investigators and scientists that would disagree with me here.

All I can say is that once again, we are still in the early phases of learning how these things work and no one has all the answers. I know many fellow investigators from all over have the problem of going into an investigation with lots of brand new batteries and coming out of it all of them drained. SOMETHING is taking that energy in a staggeringly short period of time. Further, the more successful the investigation as far as collecting information and data, the more dead batteries left in its wake.

The relatively new Portal box, which can be plugged in in

order to maintain electrical power, is also a great device for allowing spirits to speak. It too, uses radio frequencies, but it has six type voices programmed into it. A child voice in male and female, a young to higher middle aged male and female voice and then older male and female voices. My colleague Michael Bill is particularly interested in the Portal and especially gifted in its use. I like it because the background radio noise is less annoying. However, each machine I have just mentioned is quite effective and can give amazingly accurate information. Ideally, a space's history is investigated ahead of hunt. In this case, information received through these "spirit boxes" can be used to help verify information, dispelling it, questioning its accuracy and seeing if the information is plausible. And sometimes, we may get sentences that are valid in terms of language, but which seem to have no bearing whatsoever on the space or situation at hand. We keep note of these, but put them on the research back burner. On some occasions the history of a space is almost impossible to research to any great extent. Fires and floods can destroy records and in some areas, buildings are/were never officially listed anywhere. Circumstances like this are where face to face interviews with not only the people who are having the problem, but neighbors, family members, town historians – to name a few – can really be invaluable. We suggest learning all you can about the building and the land it sits on BEFORE undertaking any investigation.

There is one exception to this. As a psychic, I DO NOT want to have prior knowledge of a building or family history before going on a hunt. I simply do not want to have what I pick up tainted by information I have been given before hand. Sometimes, I can pick

up pretty much what research has already informed the group about. Sometimes I can add to it. Sometimes I get information that keeps completely counter to or unrelated to what has been learned. Often, eventually all the pieces, even those that seemed most disparate do tie together. Sometimes they do not. It is wise to keep it in your files on cases anyway.

There are one or two essential lessons to keep in mind when dealing with the paranormal. These things are especially true when you do not yet know what you may really be facing.

NEVER INVESTIGATE A PARANORMAL ISSUE ALONE.

This may be difficult. If you live alone and something is manifesting in your home, you will probably find yourself contending with it by yourself. Ideally, do not engage with it by yourself. Ask an understanding friend or family member to join you and then the two of you can do a few things more safely together. If you are interested in investigating a space that is not yours, it is essential you not explore on your own. Abandoned buildings can be structurally unstable and you could be physically hurt if a floor gives way or a piece of ceiling or wall falls onto you. You might think your cell phone keeps you in touch with help. Ideally, it would. However, if you are unconscious, you can't call anyone. Further, many older buildings that have been abandoned are veritable dead zones for cell reception even if they aren't in remote areas. A cell phone is also an extraordinary container of battery energy. If there is paranormal activity taking place, the entity may quickly drain your phone's battery in order strengthen

itself. Of course, there are also safety concerns regarding whether the property you are entering is private property and someone could show up believing you to be a potential thief or vandal. State laws vary, but you face repercussions ranging from possible arrest to being shot. In addition, remember if it attracts you and you believe no one is there, plenty of other people probably have the same thought. You do not want to wander into a conclave of homeless people anxious to protect each other and their belongings. There could be criminals just hanging out waiting for people like you to stumble into something for which you were absolutely not prepared. At Darklight Paranormal we have come across enough horror stories about people being hurt trying to do an investigation, but ultimately having nothing to do with the paranormal, that we can't stress this enough. Just do not investigate alone.

There are safer and less safe tools to employ if you want to attempt to make contact with the entities in a space. EMF meters which measure Electromagnetic Fields, not only let us know about areas where there are unusually high levels of electromagnetic energy, but can, because of the way they light up, be used to have some contact with other worldly beings rather safely. The same is true with equipment such as EVP recorders which I mentioned earlier. I cannot guarantee that the responses you hear, if you receive any, will be satisfying or comforting. They may in fact be disturbing. However, as a form of communication unto itself, Electronic Voice Phenomena recorders are rather safe. The same is true for the other instruments I mentioned earlier; SB-7 or SB-11 boxes, Ovulis boxes, Spirit boxes once again, are capable

of bringing information you may not want to hear. They are otherwise though, rather safe. There is more disagreement among ghost hunting groups as to whether the newer Portal box may be a capable of allowing spirits to actually come through the device and actually take up a stronger presence in a space. Personally, my suggestion is to always be aware and vigilant when using any devices which enable and intensify the voices and perhaps physical abilities of nonhuman beings. That said, I have been privy to many Portal sessions, as I said, Darklight Paranormal's lead investigator, Michael Bill, who is one of the most thorough and careful Investigators I have ever seen is quite well versed in the workings of the Portal and has used them literally thousands of times. He believes the device to be no more likely to give greater energy to any entities than any other electronic device.

Less scientific ghost hunting devices include items such as dowsing rods, compasses (yes, regular compasses such as you use camping, etc. They react to electromagnetic fluctuations and are a very legitimate tool if you don't have the money for an EMF meter or don't happen to have one handy) crystal or metal pendulums and the ever-popular Ouija board. What most people are not aware of is the theory behind which each of these items work. This information is very important in order to make an informed decision about which, if any, you might want to use. Generally, it is believed that dowsing rods and pendulums work through the user's subconscious. In other words, dowsing rods, which are enormously popular all over the world for finding water (the way they were originally brought to people's attention) and other things such as advantageous places to build a home or

office building or rent space in a building, etc. Theoretically, they bring to the surface information we already are connected to and help us make decisions once we have that information in front of us. These have been used in one form or another for probably over a thousand years.

Originally, they were "Y" shaped pieces of wood used by people (generally women, but that depends on the culture of the group employing what they would often call the 'Water Witch'). The 'Water Witch' may have been a bit mysterious to the community at large, but like folk healers and shamans, they performed an invaluable service. Any group looking to settle an area needs fresh, clean water. These people would help find it with their 'Y' stick or dowsing rod. Today, in some countries dowsing rods are so serious a part of daily life and decision making they are made in a variety of ways including rods that collapse into the approximate size and shape of a ballpoint pen. This way, they can always be on hand. Dowsing rods are now also used in ghost hunting. Here, the person working with them is usually someone with some level of psychic ability who can work with the rods to receive answers about whether an area, building, home, etc. contains unusual levels of certain energies. Beyond that, they can point attention to a spot in an area where a spirit may be. If asked appropriately, the spirit may use the rods to acknowledge its existence in the space and, on occasion it may move the rods in a specific way in order to answer particular questions. In my experience, this can be effective and accurate information. It does seem to deplete the entity making contact of energy. Thus, sessions of this sort rarely last very long.

Semiprecious stone or metal (usually brass) pendulums theoretically work in very much the same way dowsing rods do. In fact, they too are used by some for the purpose of finding water. Pendulums can be harder to use for many people. One has to develop their own communication with the pendulum (stones especially as they are living items that give off a vibration). However, for some people, myself included, pendulums were probably the first device outside my own senses I learned to use to do readings. While I do not use them much these days, I still enjoy them and I like them because I have only ever had positive experiences with them. For that matter, while I do not feel the same connection to dowsing rods (and that is an entirely subjective feeling, it in no way is meant to indicate one's superiority over the other).

Then we have the notorious Quija board. These are generally considered to have appeared and started to be used in the latter half of the nineteenth century during the rise in popularity of the Spiritualist movement. The theory of the way a Ouija board works is entirely different from that of the pendulum or dowsing rods. The whole concept of the Quija board from the earliest information we have about it is that it was to connect directly with the dead. And with a variety of written words and phrases as well as all the letters and numbers of the English language it provides an opportunity for the user(s) of the board to get very specific answers to their questions from loved ones or trusted ones on the other side. The problem is that most people do not know how to properly use a Ouija board. In addition, most paranormal investigators agree, even when one does know how to properly

use the board, there are still potential problems that can come up based on the very theory and concept of how it is supposed to work in the first place.

People calling on the dead who are not familiar with the proper techniques for doing so means that while we may ask to speak to a particular person, there is no guarantee that person will be the one whose spirit comes through the board. Further, most people have no way of really knowing whether they are communicating with their desired person or not. Why? One thing most investigators agree on is that people's characters do not, as a rule change after death. (There are exceptions to this which I will address a little later in this book, but for now let's work with the idea that people's characters really do not change that much after death). Most significantly the idea that people's basic core characters do not change means two things must always be taken into consideration where answers from a Quija board are involved.

The first thing to remember is that people who were attention seekers in life, are probably still the same in death. These spirits will say anything to keep the attention on them and the conversation going. Think about this carefully. It means these spirits will take any opportunity to make contact. In life, most of us avoid such characters like the plague. In death it should be no different except that they may diffuse their true colors in order to have contact and conversation. They lie. They size up their audience and figure out what they want to hear and give it to them. That doesn't sound so bad, does it? YES, it is. As with any living person who pretends to be someone/something they are not in order to get in the good graces of a person or group,

sooner or later keeping up the façade becomes too difficult. It becomes too irritating for the spirit. Their personality starts to take a noticeable turn. They are no longer showing much interest in being helpful and are far more focused on getting the same messages they spewed in life – the same ideas that made them unlikeable or unpopular and which made them appear hate filled, bitter, manipulative or otherwise dangerous – begin to show up more and more while the personality that initially drew in the people or person using the board starts to vanish. There is an especially dangerous situation here when this circumstance arises because if interest in the board started with a group, sooner rather than later the group dwindles down. Most lose interest and go on to other more pressing practical life matters. Often, that leaves one individual who feels the person who best understands them and cares most for them is a dead person to whom they speak only through the board.

This is very likely what the entity wanted from the beginning; it identified the most vulnerable person in the group and gave them what they wanted. By the same token, as it showed its true self more and more to the original group of board users they did what people do with someone like that in life. They got irritated, distracted by more pressing matters in their lives and walked away. Often, there is one person who just cannot do that. They refuse to see what the entity is really doing or saying and often choose to spend hours alone with it rather than in the company of the living. Younger people, teenagers going through a hard time at school, kids away at college for the first time (a perfect situation for an opportunistic spirit because there are few people around to

make a definitive demand to stop the behavior, again they'll most likely leave the person alone with their spirit and board than do battle with something they do not understand). Other people often vulnerable to this are people who have changed jobs and find themselves in a new city or maybe they have started their first job out of high school or college and are feeling alone. People who lose their partners to break ups or death suddenly can fall pray to this. I think you, the reader, can see where I am going here.

The more attention and energy a person gives the spirit with the board, the more energy the spirit takes in and uses to grow stronger. In some cases this can lead to physical manifestations of various sorts. Doors opening and closing with no explanation. Items being moved, hidden or broken. Unexplained voices in the house, apartment or wherever the person has been conducting the sessions with the board. The person may start suffering nightmares, have trouble sleeping, have difficulty eating. Often they isolate themselves completely from people and activities they used to enjoy. They can become severely depressed and one of the worst parts about this is that the one being who has been their best friend and confident for possibly months is now the very source of their depression and possibly oppression. We will discuss Oppression later. The person now fears this being and fears equally strongly they will be told they are crazy for what they now believe is happening and/or they were stupid not to recognize it was time to put the board down when everyone else originally interested got tired or annoyed by it.

I want to be certain to put this in proper perspective for everyone. I am NOT saying all interactions with Ouija boards will

absolutely result in this sort of problem. Many people use Ouija boards successfully and in a healthy way and find them to be excellent tools for certain kinds of psychic medium (psychics who have the ability to connect with the dead) work. I will say here is a perfect example of our Michael Bill's Ghost Hunting 101 lesson – **Do Not Hunt Alone**. Even if the hunting is in the apparent safety and comfort of your own living room or bedroom. In the case of Ouija boards, better to have more people using them as the more energy to combat anything inappropriate that comes through, the less difficult it is to shut down the session. And please, if you do want to work with a Ouija board, please talk to a professional who knows about their proper use, how to have the best outcome trying to speak to a specific spirit (with Spirit boards you never want to ask an open ended "Is there anyone here who would like to communicate?") Trust me. There will be, that's no guarantee they have anything to say you want to hear and getting rid of them at the end of a session can be a real problem. So please, talk to someone at your local occult or metaphysical shop, they should be happy to answer serious questions. If they are not, try another shop. If you do not live in an area with an open occult community and no such shops are nearby, one thing the internet is great for is listing real brick and mortar shops where real people who truly know what they are talking about are more than happy to answer your questions.

Read about Ouija board use first. Not on the internet, but in real books people have written that have been published and edited and proofread for accuracy. Thus far, for reasons most of us do not fully understand, the internet is a cesspool where legitimate

occult information is concerned. Of course, if you find good titles on line, such as on Kindle or another ebook platform, that is fine. It's the stuff anyone can put out there that is dangerous. People's agendas range from wanting to get their names out whether they have any idea what they're doing or not, to actively wanting to know they're hurting people with all sorts of things in between. Talk in person or on the phone to a professional. Almost any occult shop will have staff with knowledge about this. You may want to speak with more than one person or shop. That's fine, the more information from people who have used Spirit boards, the better. Just please, learn about them before jumping in and trying to work one. They are much more complicated than the game companies that manufacture them realize or at least, than they let you know.

Essentially, the theory is that Ouija boards, in a way unlike most other ghost hunting devices, open a door or "portal," as it's generally called, to the other side. Some people believe it opens ways to all kinds of other worlds. For our purposes, we'll focus on the concept that Ouija boards open gateways to the other side where the dead and those spirits of the underworld reside. That door is easily opened and not so easily closed. Once open, that portal is just an open doorway through which any dead spirit or even demon can easily enter our realm. Think of the potential for problems as starting in this way. Imagine you gave a party and one of your guests (invited directly or by way of being a directly invited guest's 'plus one.') Then imagine through the course of the gathering this person gets entirely out of hand. They are picking fights with your other friends, you think they're stealing things,

~ 29

they've broken an object or two and it becomes imperative you ask them to leave. Like most people who would behave that way in anyone else's home, they do not just quietly walk out. They argue with you, scream at others, blame everyone else. You finally get them out on your own or by calling the authorities. Everyone else is stunned at this person's behavior. Then, after all you had to deal with and everything your other guests witnessed, a few weeks later another of your acquaintances has a party and winds up inviting this same problem person in spite of all the problems they made at your party just a short time ago. You are left wondering what in the world your friend is thinking to open their door to this person when they witnessed or at least heard about their atrocious behavior in your home. There are fools who will do this for fun or to "see what will happen."

It never ends well. People can knock themselves out removing a malevolent spirit or worse, a demon from their abode. Finally, it has to leave. Then, some other fool goes and invites them back. They'll take advantage of the opportunity. I cannot describe to you the frequency with which people (generally young males between the ages of 16 and 25, this is an observation, not a judgment) come into our shop wanting to by books that teach the summoning of demons. We will usually refuse sale to them if they appear too anxious. Many times we will ask directly if they intend to read the entire book before embarking upon wrecking havoc. Frequently, they are honest enough to admit they do not. We will try to educate them about the potential dangers of what they want to do. There are other, better and healthier ways to release anger or do whatever they want to do which has led them

to believe summoning demons is the approach to take. Sometimes we reach these people. If we do not, we tell them to find the book elsewhere. That may sound like a harsh policy, but you see, once they create their mess – all on their own – we (my husband and I and any staff members of our shop, Starling Magickal Occult Shop in New Orleans and/or me and my partners Michael Bill and Rob Pryor of Darklight Paranormal, New Orleans) will be the ones who receive frantic phone calls at all hours asking us to come to wherever they are and put ourselves in jeopardy in order to "turn it off." We taught, explained, warned, gave alternatives; we will not at that point dig people out of the messes they knowingly, willfully and deliberately made.

Suffice it to say, Ouija boards are not for everyone, should be approached with caution, are not a harmless game, should only be used after one has learned about the theories behind how and why they work and should always be used with caution. Yes, some people can use them safely and successfully. Almost anyone like that with whom I have ever spoken STILL say they approach each session with special preparation and ready to close the session down and do ceremony to close any portal that may have been opened. The average potential Ouija board user does not have this background or knowledge and without these things, the Ouija board experience is likely to be at best an unpleasant one.

This is a perfect time to explain the difference between a malevolent spirit and a demon. First, relax, actually confronting a demon is EXTREMELY rare. Malevolent spirits are fairly common on the other hand. Further, as they are malevolent, if you ask, or a professional investigative team comes to your home and

asks this entity for its name, what does an angry being who wants attention and to get a rise out of its audience do? It calls itself a demon or the devil. In our experience and the experience of many other Investigators we know, just because something calls itself a demon does not mean it is one. Or that it is the devil. I will speak further on this shortly, but one thing that is very important to keep in mind is the following. As a rule, commonly held belief is that ghosts or spirits are attached to places.

The Catholic Church's official policy on Christian demons is that they attach to people, not spaces. They want souls or bodies, not real estate. The Catholic Church is also extremely reticent to say a situation is the work of the demonic. If enough priests agree there is something supernatural going on, they must still go to their higher ups with all their documentation on the case and after those people study the information, if *they* are also convinced there is something truly paranormal going on, they often must then approach people even further up the ladder of the Church hierarchy. In general, the case is supposed to go all the way to the Vatican whose decision is final. This process takes months, if not longer and it is not shocking to hear that the decision is that there is still not enough evidence to merit an exorcism. There are, however, a few caveats here. Catholic priests have been known to take it upon themselves to exorcise people if they have been privy to enough behavior to convince them the person is in serious danger and the ritual must be performed immediately. They have also been known to exorcise houses/buildings when an official House Blessing has proven ineffective. The Church sanctions House Blessings and which are usually performed very

quickly after they are requested. These are so common in fact, many Catholics have them performed as a matter of course when they move into a new home or business space and sometimes once a year or so to keep the energy positive.

Can A Person or Item Be Haunted?

For those who are not from a Catholic background, such as myself, let me explain something you may be wondering about. In Christianity, demonic possession is a Catholic thing. Other branches of Christianity believe in evil and demons, but feel they do not possess people in the same way the Catholics do. Thus, in theory, a Methodist minister, Protestant priest, etc. will never perform an exorcism. They will tell you they do perform House Blessing ceremonies however, which is in keeping with the edicts of their sects. However, the world of paranormal investigation and ghost hunting has become something of an industry for churches as they find their memberships, particularly the Catholic Church, dwindling considerably over the past ten years or so. This means finding a willing clergy member of almost any organized sect of Christianity is becoming easier and easier to do. They may ask outright payment, they may work by what is likely to be a substantial donation or, they may just want to get as much publicity out of the ritual as they can.

So, if someone believes they need or their family believes they need a Catholic exorcism, but they do not believe they have the time to wait for the Church to sign off on the ceremony or they do

not wish to risk the Church's refusal to do so, there are now many other alternatives. There are ministers of all sects of Christianity now taking on the responsibility of exorcising people. And, if you cannot find one of those, all is certainly not lost. There are a variety of people who call themselves things such as, "Church Sanctioned Demonologist/Exorcists," implying, at least, that they have the Church's authority to do these rituals. In some cases this is apparently legitimate, in some cases not. Keep in mind it is also widely known that the Catholic Church does actually perform far more exorcisms each year than they admit to. How they choose who to work with while avoiding the rigors that the rite is supposed to demand before it is performed is a question to which I have yet to find a consistent answer. It seems to vary depending on country and localized beliefs in those countries.

Money appears to play a big role. In some cases, it seems some priests earnestly believe this is what they were called to the Church to do. Still, if you or someone you know truly believes they or a loved one needs an exorcism NOW and none of the church associated people such as these can be found, there are all sorts of other people who claim to be specialists in this areas. Some have large followings and are very popular with those who claim to have been helped. There are many names for these people; Deliverance Ministers, Lay Demonologists Ordained as Exorcists, Ordained Exorcists – the list and terms go on. What these terms mean is that these people are people who may or may not be sanctioned or ordained by the Catholic Church to perform Exorcisms. All of them claim they are capable of performing this rite. Apart from their not otherwise being Catholic priests, the

difference between one of these people and a priest or bishop in the Church ordained to perform the ritual of exorcism is that as a rule these people do this work for money. At of the writing of this book, I have yet to come across anyone who has worked with any of these sorts of practitioners.

I imagine as with any "industry" some of these people are properly skilled and some are charlatans. I was profiled on an episode of National Geographic's "Taboo" a few years ago in an episode of the show called, "Odd Jobs." The segment on me was on my work as a Vodou Priestess, another segment on a person with an unusual occupation was on a man who performed exorcisms. If I recall correctly, he worked by donation, had repeat clients (which does bring to the fore the question of whether he's really doing exorcisms or gestalt therapy of a sort) and did the work because he felt a calling. He may really be on to something. As the membership of the Catholic Church dwindles, no doubt in large part due to the problems they have had with pedophile priests and their poor handling of these situations over decades as well as rules for behavior that more and more people find antiquated and alienating, the demand for exorcisms and Exorcists is rising dramatically. Ordained ministers of almost every faith are getting into the work. There are stories (again, I have not personally dealt with anyone who has experienced any of these first hand) of various priests and ministers, even nuns, performing Exorcisms via telephone, facetime, Skype, etc. The people performing the rituals may or may not be legitimate, the demand is very real.

Adding additional confusion to this complex issue is that many Christian clergy including Catholic priests will say that

ANYONE who is "pure of heart" is capable, if absolute need be, of performing the rite of exorcism. It's only if one really wants it conducted by an ordained Catholic priest that all the rigors the Church has officially laid out must be satisfied. One must either have a truly unshakable faith or be a fool to take this on alone. At the same time, desperate people will do anything to stop the suffering or torment of a loved one. In my own experience I will say I have been part of two true exorcism ceremonies in my life. One was of a space and dealt with a Christian demon we identified. My brother, a practitioner of European Witchcraft, Ceremonial and High Magick and Native American spiritualities participated. My husband who is very well versed in almost all religions and especially familiar with Ceremonial and High Magick took part and obviously, I did as well. My background is strong in many things. I too am very familiar with Ceremonial and High Magick, Native American spiritualities and in my case, African Traditional Religions, for me particularly, New Orleans style Vodou. (The existence of this form of Vodou is, for some, a controversial subject. I am not going to lay out an argument for its legitimacy here. There is no need to go into a topic that can potentially generate volumes of books itself). The significant matter is that both rituals were successful although the one to rid a very old African statue of spirits which someone had trapped in it required several rituals.

To further complicate matters for paranormal investigators and lay people alike, keep in mind there are demons from religious systems other than Christianity, some of whom date back far beyond the birth of Christianity. It is important to know *what*

demon you may be dealing with, if it is one at all. It is wise for any paranormal investigative team to have a good general knowledge of various regions and, ideally, an Occult specialist on the team. For Darklight Paranormal, I am the general Occult expert. Michael Bill grew up Catholic, is a priest in Haitian Vodou (my practice is New Orleans Vodou, just to clarify) and he has studied Catholic demonology while I have familiarity with a variety of pantheon's demons or dark beings. Also, there are cases of what have generally been agreed upon by professionals to be spirits, not demons of any sort, attaching themselves to people and following them from one place to another. The argument could be made here that this is in fact a misdiagnosis of a demon and that is certainly possible.

The thing to keep in mind is that in the last 150 years we have come a long way in understanding many things about supernatural/paranormal phenomena scientifically, nevertheless, the exploration is still in its infancy. There is still far more we do not know than that we do. So, while the Catholic Church officially states demons become attached to people, presumably to take over their souls, and do not become attached to places, we have plenty of information that counters this. There are cases, even some in which the Catholic Church has been involved, in which what was agreed to be thought a demon was attached to a space and left alone anyone who left the space. By the same token, ghosts are supposed to attach themselves to places, not people. The problem is there are numerous places where the same ghosts have been seen. Famously, Marilyn Monroe's ghost has been seen in several different hotels by hundreds of people over time. That's just her

favorite hotels, sightings of Ms. Monroe have been recorded in many additional places.

Then, there are recorded cases of ghosts attaching to people and following them from one place to another. Sometimes they are frightening and truly seem to wish to "haunt" an individual in the worst sense of the word. Sometimes they seem more protective. I personally believe a ghost can appear in a place it never set foot in life in order to connect with someone, particularly a family member. I was born and raised in New York City and my father died there long before I ever considered moving to New Orleans. He didn't even know of any interest I particularly had in New Orleans. Yet, on three occasions my father has made contact with me in my New Orleans home. Twice, I heard his voice out loud call out to me and the first time he made contact was through the landline telephone we had at the time.

Fortunately, my husband was with me to witness that experience. The phone rang very late at night, we were up, but I let the machine answer. We both heard what we each identified as my father's voice ask for me by name and then the connection went down. When I checked the number that had recently called, the phone had registered someone had called but there was no number or message, such as "Unavailable" or "Private Number." Nothing. According to the phone company and manufacturer of the phone at the time, that was not even possible. Further, particularly strange was that his voice had been recorded by the machine. We played it back several times to make sure we both really heard what we thought we did. Careful not to erase the message and with no one else in the house, we went to bed. The

next day while the record of a call from nowhere still existed, my father's message was gone.

As I have already mentioned, I have dealt with haunted objects personally. In my experience, only once was there a serious or what appeared to be a potentially dangerous problem associated with the item (the antique spirit doll from what was at the time of its creation the Bocongo region of West Africa). We have an ever growing collection of haunted objects. Some more troubled than others, but kept in the proper way and blessed periodically, they cause little difficulty now. Of course, they came to us because they were causing someone else a problem by which they felt overwhelmed.

Always keep an open mind and remember the rules those of us interested in the study of the paranormal are taught are constantly changing as science finds new ways to capture evidence and help prove or disprove things. We are in the infancy of study on this subject, if even that far along. Perhaps we're better off considering ourselves still in an embryonic state. Different people find different, often conflicting approaches work for them in their situation and there are few absolutes. We compile as much information as we can on which we all generally agree and then use that as a template for our work.

You may think your home, business or some item around which you find yourself spending time is haunted. There are times in many people's rental or ownership of an apartment or house or business space that unusual and perhaps, at least at first, unexplainable things which appear to be supernatural in nature occur. By and large there IS a logical explanation. A window

~ 39

slightly out of alignment may be capable of causing sounds that sound like strange other worldly whistles or voices coming into a space. Air conditioning systems in need of even mild maintenance can sometimes cause all sorts of strange sounds, cold or hot spots and electrical problems. I am reminded of one of my favorite examples of something appearing to be a paranormal issue which really was not. Many years ago, my attorney at the time contacted me very concerned about extremely strange occurrences going on in the family home. There was particular distress because they had a small child and had seen enough movies about paranormal events to know children can be susceptible to especially scary things. Actually, this child was not bothered in the least and the parents wanted to keep it that way. At all hours of the day and night the lights and television were coming on and going off all of their own accord. The air conditioning would seem to shut off on its own. Yet, no breakers were ever found tripped. The child was too young to be able to even reach light switches and the like without assistance. The refrigerator would make odd sounds and stop running. The family was scared. I knew about the house, though I had never been physically. I stopped my attorney and said, "It's not anything ghostly. You don't have to worry about that. You do need to get an electrician to your house quickly. Your house juts out into water. I can psychically see some insulation on wiring which has worn away. When the higher tides come in or the water is choppy, it splashes on the exposed wires and things in the house are effected.

I gave the exact location under the house where I saw the exposed wires and suggested the electrician look at all the wiring

under the house as some other areas felt to me as though they might be close to the same condition. While electricity and water are a notoriously bad mix, there are electricians specially trained for this kind of underwater work. I recall saying, "I know you will have someone who specializes in this, but I don't envy them." I felt someone getting a shock. The technician went out to the home, as I recall, put on some kind of special wet suit for the work and proceeded to swim under the house. He did indeed find wires with insulation that had worn away right where I said they would be. Additionally, there were some other wires that needed attending to before they became problematic as well. He worked to put everything in order. Unfortunately, during the course of the repairs, he did manage to make an error in his own safety calculations and received a nasty electrical shock. I felt it psychically before he had even gotten to the house, it was not a pleasant experience. Nonetheless, though he did require medical attention, the family if not the electrician himself were prepared for this given what I had told them.

The work was completed and the mysterious and scary light and appliance behavior ceased. I was happy to have been consulted and though very sorry for the poor man who received the electric shock. I was delighted everything wound up being repaired and fine and I was able to calm the family's fears early in the process. I was even happier that I was able to prevent a potential fire in the house which was my great concern. As I mentioned earlier when talking about not going ghost hunting alone, sometimes the paranormal investigative teams help ward off other kinds of dangers for people when we get contacted, not only ghostly

concerns. Often, we find and alert people to very real, though mundane, dangers. That is rewarding too.

Let's say you are hearing voices in your home when no one else is there or that do not belong to anyone in the space. Perhaps footsteps are being heard in rooms where there are no living people. Maybe electrical appliances and lights are going on and off by themselves. Maybe items in the home or business are going missing only to show up again later in places no one would have put them. (This is an issue known generally as "A-porting." Teleportation or teleporting is when a *human* has the ability to move objects without touching them). If you are living or working in a haunted or paranormally active location, these are all things you might easily find yourself and family members, friends or coworkers experiencing. Other common phenomena are smells throughout the space. Anything from cigarettes or cigars when there is no one around who smokes them, to particularly perfumes or colognes no one there wears. Cooking smells may be experienced. Kitchen or bathroom cabinet doors may be opened when no one was in the room to open them. Items may suddenly fly off shelves, perhaps break. Of course, apparitions may be seen. Anomalies known as "Orbs" (balls of light) or other strange visages may be witnessed by the naked eye or may not have been visible to the naked eye, but appear in photographs later. Unexplained music, singing, conversations, banging or other sounds may be heard. Sometimes there are doors that open or close by themselves and more than one person who has lived with a haunting has been temporarily locked in a room with no explanation. This is very scary. Water faucets have been known to turn on inexplicably. Marks on floors,

walls or ceilings may appear.

I have known of several cases in which the names of people in a place have been written in shaving cream or lipstick or steam on bathroom mirrors and similar surfaces Sometimes, there are full messages, sometimes only part of a name. Furniture can rattle. Animals can react strangely often refusing to enter certain areas where they may once have happily trotted around. These are things seen rather commonly. Not necessarily all in the course of one case (thank goodness!) but any number of these can be experienced, frequently several things at once. The list of unusual activities is certainly not limited to these things only by any means, but these are all fairly common. Each on its own may be explained by something that is not at all paranormal or other worldly. The more things like this that occur in the same time frame, the more likely it is something unusual is going on.

Still, if you experience a few peculiarities (particularly if they involve electrical or plumbing issues) the first thing you need to do is have the situation checked by a licensed electrician or plumber. Most paranormal investigators are not either of these and will want to make sure your space has received a clean bill of health from professionals before they will come in and start looking for anything. This is to save time as well as for YOUR safety. No one wants you to have a fire and possibly lose your place or worse, you or a loved one get hurt because you didn't take regular practical precautions. At the same time, there are cases (we had one in our own home which is haunted – more on that later) in which there is a physical problem with plumbing or wiring, however how it came to be is a mystery even to the

professionals. They can diagnose and repair the problem and tell you if it seems unusual in any way. Should that be the case, you know the problem has been recently rectified and that it was unusual.

That will help any investigators. For example, in my own home in the winter of 2017 we had a problem in one bathroom in which a pipe broke and water spewed out and caused a small flood before it was discovered and the water turned off at the source. The next day when the plumber came out with our contractor, who works largely on French Quarter buildings in New Orleans and is aware of the history of our home specifically. The plumber was a baffled. The obvious problem was that a connection between two relatively recently replaced pipes had come apart allowing the water to escape. This is not unusual except, as I said, that the pipes were fully replaced only about two years earlier. Still, things can happen. What was really odd was that where the connection had come undone one pipe screwed onto the next. But, these pipes had not only come undone, the threads of the area where they joined were sheared, flattened in spots. It looked, as the plumber put it, "As though someone had taken hold of each pipe and just pulled them apart." The problem was that the pipes were fluxed and soldered as well as screwed together. What the plumber could not imagine was what could have caused this. He commented that while it looked as though a human had pulled the pipes away from each other, no human he'd ever seen would be capable of such a feat of strength. In this case the angle at which the two pipes sat would have made it pretty much impossible to get proper hold of the pipes to pull them apart, even if there were some super

person out there who could pull two metal pipes apart through the threads, flux and solder. The problem was repaired rather easily, but when that plumber left he was definitely perplexed. My contractor and I were somewhat amused. But the information let me know, and the people leading the investigations taking place in the house nights be aware, that there had been unusual activity associated with the event.

Alright, as this point your home or building has been checked out by the right professionals and you know everything is in good, safe working order. Still, you and others are noticing unusual activity which cannot be explained is continuing. Perhaps the electrical issues or faucet problems have not changed. That IS unusual. You may need to get the professional back to double check or get a second to give another opinion. This is a good idea, but let's assume everyone at this point agrees all work is done and was performed appropriately. If the anomalies continue, this may well indicate a problem of a supernatural nature.

Here I want to address a situation that often comes up for people facing the paranormal. If you and others in your home or place of work are all seeing, hearing, otherwise sensing unusual other worldly activity, this does not apply so much to you. However, it is not unusual for activity to manifest but, at least in the beginning, only one person seems to be experiencing it. If you live alone this can be particularly unnerving, but if you have other people around who never see or hear anything out of the ordinary that is, in a way, worse. People who are the lone witnesses of activity are often made to feel silly or isolated. Worse, they can be accused of having a wild imagination, told they're under too

much stress or depending on the people around them, it may be suggested or said outright that they have a "mental disorder"or they are going "crazy."

This only adds to the sense of strangeness about the incidents and makes them scarier for the witness. That is a recipe for all kinds of emotional upheaval that need not be endured by anyone. Do not let yourself be bullied by humans, spirits (or both) into believing there is something wrong with you because you are experiencing things in a place where others are not. Obviously, if you live alone, ask a trusted friend or friends to come spend some time with you in your space. They may experience exactly what you have. If not, do not despair. When only one person is aware of strange events and other people are in the same area not hearing or seeing anything, that can be helpful information. If you have a pet or pets, watch their reactions to the things you perceive. When a manifestation seems to be taking place, take note – is your dog or cat watching the area in which you sense activity? Are they happily sleeping or doing their own thing? In my experience, dogs, cats and other mammals such as ferrets, pick up on unusual energy very quickly and will give clear and obvious reactions to it. Horses are also very sensitive which is major if the activity occurs in a barn or on a farm. Birds, even snakes can act out of the norm when something supernatural is around. They may appear afraid, bark, meow or whimper. In my own home, our spirits are very protective of us. Our animals are rarely bothered by their presence. If something new arrives, the animals are often quick to know and their behavior alerts us. But, on occasion, it has happened that we sense nothing unusual or new and one, but

only one of our animals has started to behave in an odd fashion. Especially if it is only one animal and the rest are unbothered, this is a good time to take the animal family member to the vet to make sure they're not expressing pain they are experiencing internally from a condition or disease. As we never want our nonhuman babies to suffer, have the animal acting in an unusual fashion checked out as soon as possible. There is a high likelihood a single animal is not reacting to anything paranormal. Help it get out of its distress. It may well be experiencing something easily treated.

Another question that comes up frequently is whether small infants can pick up on unusual activity. Babies and toddlers can be very open to the presence of spirits. If your infant is reacting to something in an unusual way and if this takes place at unusual times such as when they would normally be asleep, that is an indication there IS something happening and that may help give your perceptions that much more validation. Toddlers can often see, even speak to beings adults cannot see or hear even if they do have a sense of a change or problem with the physical environment of the home. This would once again validate an individual adult's sense something is off. The first thing I suggest (and this is true of probably the majority of paranormal Investigators I have come across) is to tell the child not to interact with the being or beings it talks about. Explain that they can tell it/them that Mommy and/or Daddy do not let them play with anyone they have not met. If they introduce themselves, perhaps that rule will be revisited, but not until then. See how the child reacts. Children with the classic imaginary friends will usually agree with little argument. If they

become fearful, exceedingly agitated or aggressively defend the being's presence that MAY (I emphasize MAY) be an indication there is an outside being around. If their attempts to protect the entity remains fervent, you may want to have your child talk to a psychologist. However, before we go there, let's get our own personal self in order. Some toddlers simply don't like being told, "No," but get used to it and move on.

Otherwise, what is true for our animal babies, is true for adult humans as well. Particularly if you seem to be the only person aware of or in any way perceiving unusual, possibly paranormal activity the same that you should do for your beloved animals, you should do for yourself. The first thing to do is to take the medical bull by the horns and get a full medical check up. Everyone should do this once a year anyway, though most people do not have them quite that often. The reason for this is that you want to rule out internal physical reasons for you might be seeing, hearing, smelling or feeling strange sensations. Any number of underlying physical problems can cause mild hallucinations of an auditory or visual nature or even cause a person to smell things that are not really there. Diabetes, hypoglycemia, even inner ear infections can be responsible. Yes, brain tumors can be a reason as well. I state this because it never fails when I explain this aspect of investigation to people that they immediately jump right to the notion that they must have a massive malignant brain tumor if they are having hallucinations. That or they are going insane. Then they are not sure which is worse and manage to work themselves into a frenzy over their own possible physical health problems before I even get a chance to get out my next

sentence.

I am writing this book in order to help people, not freak them out. Even many brain tumors are NOT malignant and ARE very TREATABLE. However, most people who are experiencing hallucinations of any kind are not doing so because they are suffering from any sort of brain tumor. Blood sugar imbalances are far more likely and those can be addressed. Certain infections can cause some of these symptoms also. Vitamin deficiencies can cause these symptoms. In addition, poisons can cause the senses to perceive some unusual things. Again, I am not implying that you are the victim of a deliberate poisoning by anyone. You may have a high amount of any number of troublesome chemicals or heavy metals among other things in your system. These can cause perceptions to be very skewed. Certain allergies can do this as well.

Obviously, illicit drugs, even ones you have used recreationally for years with no unwanted side effects can suddenly start to cause problems (this is not a judgment, simply a statement of fact). By the same token, many medications can cause these kinds of problems. Again, it could be a medication that you have taken for years and has now lost efficacy or your system is reacting to it differently. It could be a new medication. Also, a possible cause of problems is going OFF any number of medications. It is also possible, depending on the person's age and family history among other factors, that they may be experiencing their first bipolar episode, their first schizophrenic episode or some other physical ailment which manifests with symptoms that effect the personality, the brain and the brain's perceptions.

Please note I do not draw a distinction between "physical illness" and "mental illness" and the latter is a term I do not often use. What we refer to as "mental illness," especially in the United States, IS illness. Plain and simple. "Mental Illness" implies one can think their way out of the sickness. That is no more true for bipolar or schizophrenic patients, for example, than for it is for people with COPD or cancer. Illness is illness. Most which negatively effect one's perceptions CAN be treated and managed. Let's stop looking at health issues as having different levels of culpability on the part of the person trying to handle them. It is not about weakness in any way. That said, the first thing to do is have a thorough check up. Make certain all blood levels are normal. If the brain is not being fed properly, it cannot process information properly. It's that simple.

A good psychopharmacologist can do really thorough tests of blood and hair as well as taking inventory of the types of symptoms you are experiencing. Yes, I suggested it. A psychopharmacologist. The word is now used more often, but if you are unfamiliar, it is a psychiatrist. A psychiatrist is a medical doctor who checks you for various brain function issues and if any problems are discovered, can help you with medication, vitamin therapy or change of diet or some combination thereof to help you feel like yourself again. This is not talk therapy. This kind of doctor is not interested in how you were toilet trained or anything of that sort. They are interested in making sure the chemistry of your brain is in balance. If there is a problem, they can diagnose and treat it and suddenly the haunting you were personally suffering leaves. This is about actual illness, not problems coping with day to day life or

a major life event. There are very important treatment option for personal issues, but is not what we are addressing here.

By the way, also know that many successful and gifted paranormal professionals suffer periodically with chronic depression and other illnesses which damage perception for a time. Please be honest with your doctor. These days there are many psychiatrists and psychologists who believe in the paranormal. Do not be afraid to communicate. If the doctor dismisses your experiences outright without testing of any kind, find another. Finding good doctors of any kind in the United States can be very difficult. It is your body and mind. Be diligent and vigilant. There are websites that have doctors who are more open to spiritual matters, word of mouth is a great resource. See if the people you know have heard about or otherwise know of a good psychopharmacologist/psychiatrist. Most paranormal investigation groups will want to be certain you are healthy before they start poking around for spirits. They will generally sit down and interview you at length about many issues in your life before undertaking an investigation. This is not due to a desire to poke into your personal life. We have other things to do and we know you have other things to do than answer what may seem like very personal questions. However, it is an essential part of doing the work properly. In addition, many Paranormal Investigation groups know of one or two psychiatrists/psychopharmacologists they can recommend if you cannot find one on your own. The latter is always preferable, however.

Assuming there are no major abnormalities found by any medical professional, what next? Well, for one thing that helps

the investigators in several ways. You've been given a full medical work up and you are essentially healthy, yet you and you alone are seeing, hearing or otherwise experiencing the signs of a haunting or paranormal activity of some sort. That's a good indicator that there is an entity of some sort causing problems. It also tells us that this energy may be of a more malevolent type. Working to effectively isolate you from your friends and loved ones is a great way to make you depressed and anxious. Negative entities feed off these emotions. Under these conditions you get weaker and more vulnerable and they get stronger. Now, we are better aware of what you are dealing with as well as what we may be dealing with. That is very important for both of us. Plus, you will have that last bit of validation to know you are not losing your mind.

    The doctors have given you a the OK. You are healthy. Naturally, you may be more than a little stressed out, but that's understandable under the circumstances. NOW you want to get insight into whatever is going on and very likely, you want it gone. Yes, there are things you can do yourself in order to attempt to remove an unwanted energy or unwanted energies from your space. When I say, you can do these "yourself," I ask you to reflect on what I said earlier about ghost hunting by yourself. Just as that is unwise for myriad reasons, so is a single handed effort to remove ghosts or spiritual energies from your home by yourself. It works best and more effectively the more energy you have. That means the more people. Safety in numbers has always been more powerful. And, while endeavoring to generally cleanse a space spiritually or remove anything unwanted from the space, it may be that when threatened, the ghost or energy will reveal

itself to others or everyone in the group. That can be very healing and helpful to the person who was thinking they were all alone in that with which they originally felt alone in dealing. That's a very positive and empowering experience.

Once you know you are healthy and your brain is functioning properly, if the issue you think is somehow paranormal continues, the next step is to research the property as fully as you can. Sometimes people buy a place and its history comes up in that process. For people renting a place this research may be a little trickier. There are times people deliberately cover up certain information about a place in order to make it more appealing. There are times it is just really difficult to find much information. It is worth exhausting all avenues. Neighbors can be an excellent source of information. If you are in a place with a scintilla of repetition for being haunted and you have not heard about it, neighbors seem delighted to tell people. Historic societies, local libraries, government agencies will all have different kinds of information that the public can access. Check out everything you can. This is useful because it you have been seeing an apparition and then see a photo or read a description of someone who perhaps lived on or died on the property, you have a much clearer, more specific idea of what is going on and with what you might be dealing. Keep in mind, some ghosts can, over time become very malevolent - almost like demons. You might find the property has a history of people using it for particular spiritual or occult purposes. That could be wonderful or problematic.

The point is knowledge is power. The more you know, the better. If you believe you know who your ghost is, you may be

able to connect with them better. It can never hurt to have as much information as possible about your place. However, just because you know doesn't always mean you are equipped to deal with it. If you have any doubts at all - consult professionals. I can not stress this enough. It is also completely acceptable to contact a few people or groups. Ask how they do their work. True professionals in this area will not have any problems telling you about how they work and why. If they talk about "commanding" or "forcing" spirits or energies to do anything, this could be a red flag. Other than making them leave, this is not the best approach when dealing with the dead. Further, if dealing with something other than the spirit of a person who has passed, you want to be extra confident these people know what they are doing.

If you are not ready yet to call professionals, but believe you have a real issue. There are simple house cleansing techniques from different spiritualities which can be very effective and may be attempted at minimal risk to your group before asking in a professional ghost hunting group. First though, let me explain something that is often overlooked by the TV shows on the paranormal which are so popular at this time. While these shows tend to focus on troublesome ghosts of the past, malevolent ghosts and/or even demonic entities (which as I stated earlier are far less common than everyone seems to think) there are other forms of energy you might see or feel which could really make you as individuals or a group question things you thought you knew about paranormal activity.

Ghosts

We have talked about ghosts but what exactly is a ghost? A ghost is generally agreed to be the spirit of a person who has died. Most paranormal researchers believe ghosts appear because of one or more of several scenarios. If they died unexpectedly, quickly and violently (that would include both a situation such as murder, a fatal accident or an illness, particularly one which came on quickly and took their live suddenly). In these cases, we have good reason to believe they do not realize they are dead and are still attempting to get assistance or do their usual routine around their home. They can become confused and therefore scared and angry when, over time, the furnishings in their home gets taken away, new people put in their own devices and furniture. Remember something we take so easily for granted now, such as a cell phone was unknown to most people as recently as 1990. These beings may be terrified. They walk through their home where there seem to new inhabitants about whom the spirit was never consulted. They knock down walls, paint things, get rid of beloved furniture and worst of all – pay no attention to the spirit when it is standing directly before them demanding answers or at least acknowledgment. They must be scared, astonished at the rudeness of these strangers in their home and then, likely a little bit angry.

Ghosts who were formally human but who know they are dead and opt to remain on our realm, at least for a while. – These are often ghosts of family members who want to keep a protective

eye on their living loved ones. As a rule they are protective and loving and can be a very positive energy to have about until they decide things are OK and they can move on.

Ghosts who have been dead a long time and attempting to tell their story, but are not being heard. – This is a problem. These tend to be ghosts of tragedy for whom death has not brought peace for several reasons. For example, a 15 year old young man who was a sweet, kind kid goes off to join the Union or Confederate Army during the Civil War finds himself barely more than a baby, away from his family and facing the reality of war and battle for the first time. Suddenly, he is hit by a bullet or cannon ball. In seconds, he is dead. No last goodbye to family or girlfriend. A battle ground burial, maybe. And he is still not totally understanding he is dead. People no longer seem to see him. They don't react to seeing him. He's seen his fallen comrades buried or their bodies taken away for burial or to be returned to their families. But, in his eyes, this does not apply to him. He isn't dead. Yet, he can't seem to really walk off of or far from the battlefield. Maybe he can get as far as a close by home that may or may not have existed during the battle in which he died. He is roaming endlessly over a battlefield once soaked with the blood of soldiers from both sides.

Now, people visit, but no one seems to see the blood. They don't seem to care. The people with homes on or near the battleground land seem disconnected. They're not listening. May I go home? Which way do I head to go back to my hometown? Are they all dead? Where are the other battalions, what has come of them? Where are the leaders? Why won't anyone answer me? Why won't anyone talk to me? What seems to happen under

circumstances like this is that a sweet, gentle young spirit has become confused and terrified. Imagine standing right in front of someone asking, screaming questions and requests for help and the person doesn't react at all? As if you don't even exist? My theory is (and many people share essentially similar opinions with minor differences one way or another) that after a period of what we in our realm would call many years the fear and anxiety about being lost starts to change the ghost. This being may start to recognize that it can't be heard or heard consistently when he speaks. But, if he pulls together enough energy, the living will notice if dishes begin flying about in the kitchen. The spirit may or may not understand the dishes can be seen breaking or broken, but he cannot be seen by the average person breaking the items. The family has a souvenir from the battle. This isn't what they believe it is. I will keep getting rid of it or moving it and they'll figure it out. But they never do.

Now, the sweet gentle young man who lost his life in battle has become frustrated. Then angry. The more he demonstrates that, the more he finally gets a reaction. The more people react with fear or anxiety, the more energy they give him and he feeds on it. This makes him stronger. But, while he can get his hostility expressed, all that original teenage fear and sweetness is giving way to abject fury. None of you will help me? I will show you what feeling helpless is! Thus easily a gentle person becomes a spirit and then an angry malevolent spirit wrecking havoc with the living. Depending on the response that level of behavior receives (which is not generally going to be positive) he may get help to move on or not. If not, the spirit may become demonic in nature.

Some belief systems say such a being could actually morph into a demon. Others, such as the Catholic Church say they cannot become demons as there are a limited number of those and they were never human. They teach humans cannot become demons. I tend to believe this. But, on a practical level, a very angry, malevolent formerly human spirit can be nearly as problematic.

What the hell was that thing?

There are other manifestations of paranormal energy one may come across which do not appear human or even look like demons in the ways we are accustomed to seeing them. There are energies known as elementals. These are basically best described as manifestations of energy which is believed never to have been human. They are manifestations of the energy of the spiritual energies of Air, water, fire, earth, even stone, wood, shell. Anything that is living non-human energy can help create an elemental. We do not know how long they have existed, though there are tales of these things going back hundreds, if not thousands of years. The holy texts such as the Bible even refer to energies which from the descriptions would seem to be Elementals. These energies are, as a rule, connected to a place and not people. However, if you are sharing your space with one, it can be very disconcerting. They do not communicate with people through language well. If an Elemental is identified in your space and causing you enough distress you want it removed, your best bet is to contact a professional Occult shop/specialist. These are

not energies easily removed by lay people.

There are other kinds of energies that can follow people or be attached to a space. They have dozens of different names and descriptions. They can appear as black balls of energy, usually no more than 1' 1/2" to 2' high. The one I have seen resembles something like a round tumbleweed. This energy does not seem to have ever been human, but does have a conscious of some kind. My brother has one that follows him only in times when he is severely stressed. This energy ball will seem to chatter very, very quickly (we have not yet had an opportunity to catch him on digital recording and slow down the sound in order to see if it is simply making noise or if it is speaking a language, but too quickly to be understood by the human ear. This energy, which we refer to as male – those who have witnessed it all just get a male sense of it – seems very protective of my brother. It allows me to see it which I believe means it does not consider me any sort of potential threat to my brother. And it is possible that it manifests from my brother somehow. These are the kinds of energies we know the least about. They seem rarely dangerous and many people find them protective and comforting. But, if you have never seen one before, they can certainly be jolting.

There are cases in which all the evidence and experience of the people living with the phenomenon speak of seeing menacing creatures in their domain. These can vary drastically in appearance according to different descriptions. There are people who insist they have seen devil-like creatures with horns, glowing red eyes, etc. However, though understandably terrifying, these beings ultimately do not really act like devils or demons. They are just

scary and nasty and do not appear very long (though the time may feel like hours while happening). People have reported seeing human-like forms which can crawl on walls and ceilings. Sometimes people see masses of black or white, very opaque smoke or mist.

In many cases this mist, once apparently aware it is being watched can morph into other forms; ghosts, something evil, even angels in some cases. From my own studies and discussions over the years with people who claim to have seen any number of otherworldly apparitions, I have come to believe most of these beings are ghosts of humans who have learned not only to appear to the eyes of the living, but have learned over time to do so while making themselves as scary to the living witness as possible. Many investigators believe some spirits develop over time an ability to tune in to the greatest fears and phobias of the living and then take on the form of what is most feared. While this is very definitely an exceedingly unpleasant ghost, it usually is a ghost. Not an actual evil entity. I can't say this knowledge makes them less frightening, but it does make the situation more manageable. These are usually found to be beings who still have a story to tell. Perhaps a murder that went unidentified or for which there was no justice. Perhaps information hidden somewhere in the building which sheds light on a situation which was very important to the person who passed. If the information can be retrieved, often these spirits, scary as they are, go away rather quickly once they have a sense someone knows and believes their story.

There are dozens of names for these kinds of spirits/beings. Many are colloquial. The legends of certain energies are well

known in the Southwest United States that are unheard of to most people in New England who have their own group of troublemakers. The Midwest United States has yet another group, the Middle to Southern Eastern Seaboard has its share. Some maintain similar traits, some do not. Names for particular, hard to categorize, entities such as these range from Puckwudgies to Goat Boys to Tommyknockers to Black Eyed Kids to dozens, if not hundreds more. I should point out that any of these phenomena along with a plethora of others too numerous to name here are all worthy of investigation on their own and each could be (and have been) the exclusive subjects of investigations and books encounters with these sorts of beings are definitely paranormal, they are rare. Further, cases of them appearing in or trying to interact with humans in places where humans regularly live and/or work are even more unusual. Because of this, I am not going to go into detail about these energies here. For our purposes, this would just muddy the waters.

Doppelgangers

Another way in which some entities can really confuse and at the same time scare people to death is by taking on the appearance of someone else living or working in the home or building or otherwise close to someone in the home. The curious thing about doppelgangers is that they usually only appear to one person at a time. In my own home building doppelgangers have appeared more than once. One time, my colleague, Michael Bill was entering

the upstairs of our back house or "dependency" presumably to prepare it for the night's ghost hunt. He was witnessed by one of his colleagues at the time who was a bit surprised he'd not greeted her on his arrival. She went upstairs to see if he was alright only to find no one was there. There is only one set of stairs and exiting the house via the balcony, though possible, would require at least three or four minutes and would be virtually impossible to do without shaking the building enough to notice something strange happening. It wasn't three minutes before Michael Bill saw his coworker had gone up the stairs and went running up after her to apologize for arriving a little late. When she told him she'd seen him and followed him upstairs he was adamant he'd only just arrived.

    Around the same time as this incident, on another evening, I saw Michael Bill head upstairs and waited for him to come back down because I wanted to check on something with him. Only about two minutes later he came in through our front gate and greeted me. This would have been completely impossible for him to do had he been in the back building. I told him what I had seen and this prompted us both to wonder what spirit was mimicking his appearance and why. I have also seen my husband in the courtyards on several occasions only to go into the front building and learn he has been very much asleep for some time. People have seen me walking around. In every case, each person was seen in the courtyard, not inside the house. There is a menacing sense to this experience. We can however, put to rest one superstition. It has long been said that when one's doppelganger is seen by themselves or anyone it is a message that person is going to die

in the very near future – usually within two or three weeks. All of these experiences took place at minimum two years ago and all involved are still very much alive. There are plenty of other cases such as this where a person's double has been seen, but they remained alive without even a dangerous incident. That should make some of you feel better.

Remember, the hard and fast rules about hauntings and spirits are not always nearly as absolute as we may have been told.

Poltergeists

Very possibly the most misunderstood of the paranormal energies (especially since the 1980s iconic movie franchise which identified their behavior incorrectly) is the Poltergeist. Literally translated, "Poltergeist" is a German word meaning "noisy ghost." In fact, poltergeists are not ghosts at all. They are paranormal energies which may certainly be noisy and disturbing, but which unlike regular ghosts (I believe in the translation the word "ghost" means something more along the lines of 'unseen force' than spirit of the dead) emanate from a LIVING source. A poltergeist is actually a manifestation of energy which may cause sounds, shaking of furniture, electrical abnormalities and other such things. But, in this case, the energy is being manifested by a living human being. You may have heard about poltergeist activity often taking place in homes in which children, generally between the ages of 10 and 15, reside. During these ages, as all of us who have passed them know, one's hormones have minds

of their own. Emotions therefore can run very high. Our bodies seem to have changed a bit more every time we wake up. We have new awareness of sexual desires and little knowledge as to what to do with them although they are extremely powerful forces and that's disturbing unto itself.

People this age may additionally be experiencing sibling rivalries, first crushes (with emotional AND sexual feelings) and quite possibly things like school problems, parents having marital problems that we don't understand and which scare us. Anyone who remembers their preteen and early teen years must remember some of the inner turmoil. Now, as with all matters, some people manage such things better than others. For certain people when all these feelings get together and are too intense for the person to know what to do with them, they tend to try and swallow them. We try to pretend nothing is wrong and go about our days as normally as possible. For a small group of those people that isn't entirely workable. The frightened and excited and overwhelmed feelings find a way to release themselves from the person experiencing them. Rarely, does the person know they are doing this and even if they do, controlling it is still an entirely different issue.

While the strange activity usually stops as puberty ends, it should be pointed out that not all people who manifest poltergeist energy are children or young teens. Adults facing extreme anger, fear, anxiety and other such major emotions can also find themselves dealing with poltergeist energy. It is rare, but again, I know from first hand experience, it can happen. Several years ago I was dealing with an injury and separate illness at the same time.

I was supposed to be on bedrest, but was unfortunately also in close proximity to some rather toxic and unthinking people who made a couple of major mistakes while I was unable to be on top of things. I thought I had left very specific instructions so, when I was made aware of the situation I would then have to spend time and energy and money cleaning up, I was about as furious as I ever remember being. I have a temper, but this was something I can't even explain. I became so livid that I actually made my whole house shake. In this event at least I knew I was responsible for doing it, but if I had been asked to do it on queue I could never have done it. People in my house at the time came running to my bedroom aware the building was shaking, unaware if I knew it was shaking. I calmed down, so did the walls. Additionally, I think everyone around me got the message. That was the most dramatic incident of it. On occasion such things have happened my whole life.

This phenomenon also falls under the term "PK" or "psychokinesis," meaning a living human who is able whether deliberately or under the right stressful conditions to move objects with their mind. Investigators of psychic phenomena may want to study people who have this ability, should they wish to be studied. Paranormal Investigators rarely study this. We may help identify it, but it is not in our skill set to help someone control it. If you or someone you love is dealing with being the creator of poltergeist activity in your home or somewhere else, the best suggestion I can give is to try and help the person stay as calm as possible. While doing that, find a good talk therapist, ideally one who specializes in people with these abilities (yes, there are

psychologists who specialize in working with people who are psychic in many ways). This will give the person skills to help them cope throughout life with their more intense emotions as well as giving them a safe place to talk about their feelings and work out practical personal problems. This approach is, in most cases of people who are in the middle of poltergeist activity, extremely effective in helping them get control over their fears, anxiety, anger, etc. and as a rule the energy manifestation can be brought to a minimum if not end. If you have someone who wants to do it and learn to better control it to suit their personal purposes, therapy is all more called for in my opinion. That is a dangerous potential behavior for the person with the capability and pretty much everyone around them. A good therapist can offer excellent alternative approaches.

I just bought a new piece of furniture or object (or such an item was gifted to me) and the entire energy in my surroundings has altered for the worse. Could this item have a negative spirit or negative energy attached to it?

Yes. Whether it is brand new or an antique, items can have negative energy or spirits attached to them. There are ways to cleanse these things and ideally, rid the piece of any unwanted energy. Fortunately, it is much easier to, if necessary, dispense with such an item or perhaps destroy it if cleansing its energy does not seem to work. I will address this shortly. The important thing to know is that objects CAN hold positive or negative energy. How that energy came to be connected with the item may or may never be known. If you bring something new into your home and notice people acting strangely, perhaps being inexplicably hostile

or arguing starting for no real reason over nothing, this would be a good indicator something is wrong. Some items can cause unexplained fear or panic attacks in people not prone to them. Sometimes a sense of darkness or depression becomes palpable, most noticeably in the room or area in which the object is kept. You can see if anything changes if you move the item to another area. Sometimes, something that simple will be the answer. Sometimes, not. If not. It's not unreasonable to think there is an issue. Note – the things most likely to cause problems by bringing unwanted attached energies with them are antique furniture or pieces such as dishes or silverware, mirrors, antique mirrors most of all, for a variety of reasons artwork and old books. Old or antique toys can be problematic as well. Obviously, this is not a complete list, any number of things may have unwanted energy connected to them.

DEMONS

A demon is a very conscious being that according to most spiritualities/religions was not ever human. One problem with the term "demon," is that people tend associate it only with the demons in the scope of the religion in which they were brought up (if they had one). The truth is there are many kinds of demons. While in the United States we tend to first think of demons in terms of Christianity and Catholicism in particular, there are many other demons. Islam/The Middle East has its own demons. Judaism has others. The Native American/First Nations people of the Americas have their own demons that vary by Indian Nation,

Tribe in that Nation and area of the country. There are demons of the Greek Orthodox faith. The American Amish have demons and concepts about demons which are other than the rest of American Christianity. There are Asian demons and what they call, "Hungry Ghosts," which are usually formerly human spirits which through a series of situations have now become demon like. There are Egyptian and African demons.

Pretty much every group of peoples on Earth has their own group of groups of demons and many of those, for instance Egyptian, Asian and African demons, predate Christianity by thousands of years. So, while Christian demons tend to get the most attention in the United States, they are not the only ones. In some belief systems demons may once have been human or even angels or deities. Generally, entities which can be identified as having lived on or near the property in question are spirits which have, for a variety of possible reasons, begun acting demonically. In other words, they mimic the behavior of demons, but do not meet the actual definition of the word according to most faiths and practices which believe in demons. This is in no way to suggest they are less frightening or not harmful. They can be. My own studies lead me to believe they are usually formerly living human spirits who have unfinished business and a story to tell and want justice or vengeance. The problem is that they have not been heard or not been heard correctly leading them to do (as I mentioned earlier) exactly what humans do under the same conditions; scream louder. Throw tantrums. Do anything to get attention.

Often, I believe they do not really mean to frighten people,

they hope to get someone to sit and ask them to calm down and explain what the problem is. But, not many people wish to take on that kind of anger and other worldly energy (and sometimes physical strength or ability to make people perceive things that do not actually exist). I have heard of cases in which very courageous people have actually successfully endeavored to "love" a being such as this into the light where it can find forgiveness to give and receive as well as peace. I think this makes a great deal of sense. It is however, not a behavior for the faint of heart and is probably best undertaken by a group with similar religious beliefs. I have found personally, that expressing to an upset spirit or group of them that while I or my people (family, friends, clients) had absolutely nothing to do with whatever terrible thing they endured, I do sympathize and if they will let me, I will try and help them move along on their journey where they should go and where they will find peace.

Almost always, if you ask a spirit if they see an area of light, they will give some indication that indeed they do. Then the question is why do they not go towards it and enter into it? From what we can tell, this seems to be something of a universal experience for going on the next step of one's soul's journey. The answers can run a fascinating gambit of reasons. The most obvious concern for many is that they believe they did something or maybe a few things in life that would make them unwelcome to enter the light. They believe they know where they would go and they have no desire to go there. These spirits can become absolutely enraged by attempts to move them on. Their fear and anger usually causing havoc. They can throw heavy objects at people and make very real

attempts to hurt them in order to make them stop. It takes skilled professionals or at the very least, people with great patience and the ability to communicate to some extent with the presence in order to truly explain the light is their to get them out of suffering, not trick them into something worse.

In these cases it is the state in which they are in between worlds which is a purgatory state. This is explainable and moving them on is, I believe, always possible. I realize some of my colleagues would disagree with me here. The truth is we have no finite or absolute answers. But, I firmly believe good always wins. Frequently people come into my shop for a consultation which often turns out to be part confession, part requests for advice as to how to make things right and then invariably the question is asked, 'Am I a bad person?' I learned long ago that some of the most preposterous, bizarre, behaviors take place between people. On paper, these actions, whatever they are, may seem outright Shakespearean in intensity or perhaps truly inappropriate or 'wrong' behavior. I have also learned that far more humans have these experiences and find themselves feeling alone and guilty and terrified of being discovered. This just makes matters worse. As a licensed and ordained Reverend in the State of Louisiana, I hold many people's secrets. I have learned that no matter what has happened there is (barring the behavior of someone with an illness such as a psychopath in which case that kind of person has no need to come to terms with their behavior, so wouldn't be contacting me) always a back story.

We're also not talking about people who have killed or committed terrible crimes of a legal sort, it is almost exclusively

matters of the heart. Someone feels hurt or unloved or unwanted and seeks comfort in the arms of someone else. They have a significant other. The guilt and confusion and upset all come into play and all kinds of trauma is experienced. But, all the wounds are real. I have yet to come across someone who has cheated on their significant other who did not try to explain they were not having their needs met in some way. Then, if the person has the opportunity to have their needs met, even momentarily, by another, the person cheated on feels generally fully entitled to their ethical ire and unfortunately often has people around them who support that. Rarely will they admit their behavior could have had any ability to alter the outcome. They are also generally always the ones unwilling to get counseling. I have seen cases of husbands married to one wife while sleeping with an ex wife. Women becoming involved with their boyfriend's brother or cousin. Situations that might seem to be especially wrought with trouble.

The truth is, people who spend the most time together tend to know each other the best. They pick up on other's wants and needs and everyone has a right to happiness. I am not saying doing anything you want is acceptable. I am saying that things happen and I have learned over the years that short of inappropriate behavior with a child or someone who cannot give consent, physical abuse or something of that nature – it really is not for any of us to judge. More to the point, people who are really thoughtless, careless, horrible people NEVER ask anyone if their behavior has somehow lowered them in the eyes of the Universe or God because the question simply does not occur to

them. And people caught in this trap in life, can remain caught in it after they pass. This is one reason I am adamant about people who want it getting talk therapy. I will not go into my opinion of the medical system in the United States or anywhere for that matter here. Nor will I rage as I could against the psychology industry in this country, except to say that helping a friend or family member without judgment can be one of the greatest gifts you can offer. The happier and more grounded people are in this world, the more easily they seem to transition into the next. It's also just more pleasant to be around people who aren't terrified or sad, isn't it? Accepting our dark sides is essential to happiness. That may still sound counterintuitive to some, even in this day and age. My experience though, tells me it is the case.

Thus, when people ask me about good and bad, right and wrong and forgiveness from the Gods I like them to know the simple story of one of my personal favorite Catholic Saints, San Cipriano. The story of San Cipriano starts with a love story. He fell in love with a woman and adored her in every way, she was everything to him. They loved each other and had a beautiful relationship for quite some time. Then, eventually, the woman began to drift away. She told Cipriano she no longer loved him and their relationship ended. She went on to another and instead of asking her what was wrong or what they could do together to get back to the place of love they had experienced, which most people would do, Cipriano became dangerously despondent. He did beg her to take him back at first (which anyone who has ever been in such a situation knows is the least appealing thing one can do if they are not offering to work on the relationship and make

changes or compromises). When that did not win her back and seemed only to push her further away, the next answer to come to him was even more ill advised. He turned to "Black Magick" to win back the affection of his lady. Again, I could discuss the many issues I and many of my colleagues in the Magickal community have with the term, "Black Magick." But, for our purposes here let's let it suffice to say the translation of the story must be considered in part and it is safe to say Cipriano turned to forms of magick considered less desirable.

Most importantly, he was probably trying to do spell or ritual work to force his beloved to give up what she was doing, the man she now lived and her new life. That is a great deal to try and rip someone away from when they are happy and it is not fair to try and damage someone's happiness. If they don't come to you on their own, let them be. If you really love them, let them be happy. Still, for a time Cipriano persisted with this approach. It is said it did nothing but make the woman stay further and further away from him. As begging had failed and then Black Magick had failed, Cipriano was left wondering what to do next. Now, his relationship with the love of his life was horribly damaged AND by his turning to the dark arts to get her back, he had broken away from God who would not help him. He tried to figure out what he could do to make things better. Then it came to him that the first thing he needed to do was go humbly to God and ask sincerely for forgiveness for turning away from the light and working in the dark arts. Immediately upon doing that, it is said God responded. God told him nothing was so terrible that he would turn away from any of his children if they saw the error of

their ways and honestly repented. Once Cipriano reconciled with God, his relationship with the woman he so dearly loved became repairable. Eventually, they reunited, married and lived the rest of their lives happily. Thus, San Cipriano is the patron Saint of Reconciliation. Reconciliation with all loved ones from God to friends, family and romantic loves. And all it really took was a simple, but heartfelt, "I'm Sorry."

I love the story of San Cipriano. It teaches us so much about our interactions with others, with ourselves and with any higher power in which we might believe. If a pure apology could do so much for San Cipriano, imagine how it might affect a spirit who has been wounded and enduring that wound for years, decades, maybe centuries. If we are not responsible for the wrong that was done, that doesn't mean recognizing the wrong and making efforts to remedy it will not go a long way toward bringing peace to a space in which peace and serenity have been sorely lacking and fear and hostility have been the norm.

Here, I will reiterate that while I hold the opinion that with enough human energy from healthy adults and enough of the proper knowledge, I believe any negative energy can be moved out of a space. Keep in mind, energy cannot be created and it cannot be destroyed, it can only change form. While a ghost may be moved along or changed essentially permanently, a demon can only be sent elsewhere (preferably back to where it came). I cannot, however, stress strongly enough that If you have any reason to believe you may be dealing with ANY kind of demon, that is absolutely NOT something you want to try and rid from yourself, a loved one or your home without the help of skilled

professionals. As I said earlier, many entities will try to get you to believe they are demons when most of the time they are nasty ghosts. You need professionals to investigate what is going on. Then, they may need to bring in an Occult specialist or specialists who might be able to identify what demonic being it may be and from what pantheon. Though demons tend to show up in the homes of people who are of the religion to which they belong, because they have the capacity to attach themselves to people for whatever their reasons, just because your family is Christian does not guarantee the demon plaguing you comes from that background.

The reason this is very important to understand is that if you go in to attack an entity as powerful as a demon or Asian Hungry Ghost, and are unaware of how many of these entities there are from how very many cultures and religions, you might start throwing around Holy Water and burning sage ad nauseam only to find that the thing(s) laugh and instead of wanting to get out, wish to stay and watch your show. There are cases in which demonic entities in the United States have been known to have sage smoking up the buildings in which they have come as though the building was on fire and having Holy Water sprayed all over enough to make a swimming pool only to have the entity convey the message, 'You do understand I was around before the whole Christian God and Holy Water thing? That won't help you here.' The being may just laugh. At worst it will get more annoyed at your inhospitable behavior and become uglier in its own actions. I can't stress enough that if you are dealing with any kind of demon, you need professionals to help. Most likely a team of them.

Now, Your home or building has received a thorough inspection and all is in order. You have had a thorough checkup with your doctor including a full blood panel, a hair test if you can get him or her to do one (that can be difficult as it is not a test most doctors do regularly) and, if you are really wise, you've consulted with a psychologist who feels you are in control of your senses and something is going on for you. A psychologist may not be able to say you are absolutely experiencing something paranormal, they can say that you are quite capable of telling the difference between real and imagined. I can't stress enough that these are not things to be uncomfortable about or in any way by which to be embarrassed. Investigators undergo these tests often when joining a group. It is part of the methodology of making certain both investigator and client have the clearest, best investigation of the unusual activity going on around them. We do it. It's wise for the client to do so as well.

The first thing to do is take all the information you have already been collecting and put it down on paper, if you have not already. Many people find they start keeping a journal automatically when they really start noticing behavior is taking place which cannot be easily explained. Note what date you first began to notice what events. Not everything is likely to have started on the same day. If you can't recall an exact date, no reason to panic, do your best to estimate when what began. Did anything start and then cease? Was any activity replaced by a different unusual one? This will help you take note of things you may not have thought about in the moment. Do the events coincide with times you or someone else in the household were especially agitated, anxious or upset

about anything beyond the things going on in your home? Do the events happen close to personal or general holidays? Does anything seem to happen consistently at a particular time of day or on a particular day of the week?

The reason this information is important is that it may help you understand better with what kind of issue you are dealing. Remember to keep aware. Does the manifestation seem aware in any way of you? If not, it is very possible that it may not pick up or change very much. There may be a specific time of day or night it is most active. This would probably have been the time it was active over and over in the past and that psychically embedded tape is repeating itself. Or possibly, the time of day or night is in itself of importance to the place and/or entity. This is another reason to learn the history of both the building and the land on which it stands. If manifestations seem strongest on particular dates, that may indicate there was always a big fuss made on Thanksgiving or Mother's Day or, if it's a date that isn't a recognized holiday, perhaps it was somebody's birthday or the day they graduated high school or college.

At this point, with some time frames to help possibly make greater sense of things, the next step you want to take is to do whatever investigating you can of the history of your space. It doesn't matter what kind of space it is; a single family home you own or rent, an apartment, condo or coop you own or rent. Buildings with businesses in them. Virtually every building has a history of some sort on file. You may want to start with Google. You may want to visit your local historical society. Neighbors can be great sources of information, but as with any time that

~ 77

deals with an eye witness or person trying to remember a (quite possibly) complex story, keep in mind details can easily become confused. Often, you might find yourself talking to the child or grandchild of a person who has passed away who used to tell the story of your place or the people who once had it and what happened to them or one of their family members. Their memories may be faulty, the story they got originally may have been flawed or incorrect in any variety of ways. However, if several people have what is largely in most ways the same story, that is helpful.

Problems can begin in a space at a variety of points. Dealing with hauntings in the Americas, particularly Canada and the United States in this case, virtually everyone is now familiar with the concept of the negative events that can take place in a building erected on a Native American burial site or a piece of ground sacred to the Native Americans. While in some ways cliché, thanks to a plethora of badly researched movies and TV shows which have come out over the past five or six decades, this can be a very powerful and sometimes very negative and frightening circumstance. But this isn't the only way land itself can be the source of a supernatural problem. Land on which any sort of battle took place (one between just two people, a small group or where part of an outright war was fought) and loss of life took place, whether in significant numbers or a single person, can be severely effected. There are cases of this all over the world. Places where bad accidents occurred and death took place shockingly and unexpectedly can absorb that trauma as well. The point is the very land on which your building was built may be the source of your paranormal anomalies. Or, contributing to them.

Let's say you are in a house or building and experiencing strange activity. While the land on which the building sits may have a terrible history all its own which might easily contribute to whatever you are dealing with paranormally, the longer the building has been there – or for that matter, any building has been on that ground – the greater the chances that the troubled energy of what happened on the land has now seeped into the building standing on that land.

A personal favorite example of this is the infamous Axe Murder House in Vallisca, Iowa. For those unfamiliar with this case, during the night of June 10, 1912 a farmer named Josiah Moore, his wife and children were all bludgeoned to death by at least one intruder. No one was ever arrested or brought to justice for the crime. No viable suspects could be found. What I have always found strange is that people rarely take note that Iowa is part of Plains Indian territory and the word "Vallisca," is a Sioux word roughly translated to mean, "Place of evil spirits." Clearly, this would indicate that this area, this land already had some kind of negative history known to the Native Americans of the area, probably long, long before the Axe Murder Farm House was ever even built.

Yet, it seems the settlers of European decent opted not to pay attention. Human arrogance can be a good friend to malevolent forces. In this case, we do not know enough to say whether the killer or killers of the Moore family had a personal grudge against Mr. Moore or his wife. The children were each quite small, so a problem with them is unlikely. So, it is impossible to say whether there was some sort of personal or business issue that inspired

~ 79

someone to commit these exceptionally gruesome killings. But, it is not unreasonable to wonder if the killer's sense of anger or having been wronged or overwhelming desire to kill might have been only a fleeting thought or fantasy and not been acted upon had the area not already been somehow marked as tainted or cursed by the people who knew it best.

In this case, when the Moores had the house, it by itself probably held no negative energy. There is no record of anything of that nature. It would seem the land on which the house was built was where the problem began. Of course, once this horrific atrocity occurred in the house on the land that was already troubled, the ghosts of the Moores have been seen and heard by paranormal investigators and lay visitors alike.

Another famous house with a layered history of trauma is the Lizzie Borden house in Fall River, Massachusetts. Virtually every American knows the story of the bludgeoning of Andrew and his wife Addy Borden and the subsequent accusations that Mr. Borden's daughter, Lizzie, committed the crimes, possibly with the help of her sister, Emma. What most people do not know is that the house had already been the site of a murder-suicide before the Lizzie's immediate family ever lived there. In fact, Andrew Borden's brother, Lawdwick Borden, had lived in the house with his wife Eliza Darling Borden. (She was one of several wives to Lawdwick). What sets Eliza apart is that some time in the 1840s (Andrew and Addy were murdered in 1892) she committed suicide on the property by cutting her own throat (at least this is the story, the exact details have proven very difficult to uncover) but not before killing two of her three children by

Lawdwick.

One has to wonder about the energy that may have been on the land at the start. Further, there are stories that Eliza Borden had started hallucinating and speaking of hearing voices telling her to kill herself and the children. Again, these are very difficult to verify, but they persist. Was Eliza demonstrating the signs of the onset of schizophrenia as would likely be strongly investigated today? It is possible, of course. However, in her thirties, she was older than most people who have their first episode of the disease. In addition, while schizophrenics often experience visual and auditory hallucinations, they very rarely become killers. Usually, they become fearful of others and death in general. It is worth noting that many investigation groups have conducted hunts in the house and while some do seem to connect with Lizzie and other members of her family, child spirits are apparently quite frequently picked up. As there were no small children living in the house at the time of the killings of Andrew and Addy, there is every reason to assume these would have been Lizzie's young murdered cousins. And, if they are active in the house now, there is no reason to think they would not have been when Lizzie was living there.

With all of this, Andrew Borden, who was notoriously cheap, opted to take this house rather than one in a better area of town which could have had some running water and electricity. This odd and arguably poor judgment does make one question what it must have been like to live with the man. Excessive August heat in New England and no cool water immediately available might drive any number of people to lose their tempers and become

violent. Though prosecuted for the killings, Lizzie Borden was exonerated of all charges. The case was never solved.

So, there you see the reasons knowing the history of the land a building sits on as well as the building itself is very important and helpful in understanding your own haunting, if you have one. The Borden story also beautifully demonstrates the importance of learning from an objective, licensed professional that if you are seeing or hearing unusual activity going on around you at home, work (or both) you rule out the possibility that there could be a physical problem with the building or a physical health problem throwing off your perceptions.

Something Unusual Is Going On~ How Do I Handle It?

Here we have a question only you and your loved ones can answer in terms of what approach is best for you to try first. I am not going to say one is right or wrong, that is really largely a matter of what you feel will make everyone in your space feel most comfortable and empowered.

You could call in a paranormal investigation group. They will (usually) be able to verify the activity, which can be priceless in terms of peace of mind for many people. When speaking to groups, be certain to ask if they are actually familiar with and capable removing any presence they might encounter. There can never be a guarantee that anyone can remove unwanted energy or energies from a space. However, some groups exist solely

to validate that there is unusual activity taking place, but have no clue how to remove it. On the other hand, some groups will simply take your word for what is happening and start doing rituals and activities to rid the space of all non living beings.

Each of these approaches is problematic. To have an objective group come and tell you, yes, there is phenomena taking place can be very reassuring. However, if they leave without DOING something about it, you have a great chance of having stirred up the energy further and perhaps upset it. In that case, problems only escalate and that helps no one. One the other hand, a group that comes in and starts trying to remove anything and everything without knowing what they're dealing with can also do damage. They too, can agitate the spirits and that is never desirable. They also may remove some spirits who were being helpful while thereby allowing the ones really causing problems to gain more strength.

One of the best examples of this I have come across was a young couple with a small baby who were being terrorized by activity in their home, some of which seemed to be very focused on the baby. On one occasion, the mother had walked into the baby's room after hearing some unusual and unnerving noises only to find the child missing from its crib. This baby was not yet crawling, let alone walking and climbing, so there was no way it had wandered out of the crib on its own. After an understandably frantic search of the house, the baby was found. It was wrapped safely in a blanket, and under the crib. The couple decided to start doing Catholic banishing rituals of the house the next day. Immediately noises got louder, things got worse. The baby was

~ 83

not found under the crib again. Now, it was being awoken at night and scratched. The parents would hear the baby shrieking on the baby monitor and run into the room to find the child standing inexplicably in the crib with serious scratches. Before the cleansing, the baby had never been heard crying, let alone screaming and had not been scratched or bruised. Only wrapped up and moved.

When I became aware of the case and consulted on it, I asked information the last group hadn't bothered with. I said that while finding your infant wrapped in a blanket and on the floor under its crib had to have been absolutely terrifying beyond belief, I was curious. It actually sounded as though someone had taken care to see that the child was warm, safe and protected from hard or sharp objects. This didn't actually sound like the work of a spirit meaning harm. In fact, it sounded more as though it was trying to protect the child and hide it from a more malevolent being. Now, with the haphazard cleansing and banishing work, it sounded to me as though that spirit took the message and left while the negative entity refused and now it had full access to the baby. I asked if given the way the child had been found under the crib, once the realization set in that it was healthy and safe, had no one considered that someone may actually have been trying to protect the child, not harm it.

The father had known his grandmother only vaguely, but thought he'd sensed her presence in the house early on. It turned out that, during World War II she'd been in hiding in Germany. There had been an incident in which the Nazis had come into the house in which another family was hiding the grandmother and

her family including a baby. It was never clear if it was the father's parent or aunt or another child. She'd wrapped up the child in haste and slid it under the crib and put some blankets in front of the child to hide it. The family hiding the husband's grandmother had a toddler, slightly large for the crib, but the Germans bought the story and left. The infant had been saved in nearly the exact way the couple's child had been found. The grandmother, it seemed, had been watching over the child at night to protect it. When it was demanded she leave, she did. The nastier entity was not so accommodating. Eventually, the unwanted energies were moved out of the house. To my knowledge, the family has had no problems since. However, had the more religiously driven group asked questions, the baby might well have been spared physical abuse.

If you choose to work with a paranormal investigation team, make sure they investigate and can make efforts to remove anything they might find.

Money

Another thing to be aware of is groups charging for what they are doing. It is perfectly acceptable for a professional to charge to come to your home, investigate it and generally cleanse and bless it if this is something you are doing as a precautionary measure. You're moving into a new place and want the energy at its best from the beginning. This is fine if there are no problems. Paranormal teams and psychics have to make their livings. If you are of the school that believes all psychics should do what they do for no

pay, that is antiquated thinking from a time when most psychics or town healers had other jobs by which they earned their living. These days psychics often make their living only working in this field. They deserve compensation. By the same token, however, few reputable paranormal Investigators will charge to come into a situation in which there appear to be serious problems or dangers As a rule, the client would pay for travel money, provide hotel or lodging costs, and costs for food. Donations after the work is done are enormously appreciated in order to continue the work. But, they are not necessary. This is something important to work out before you have a team to your place.

Your Space Has Been Checked, There Are No Electrical Problems And Your Health Is Fine - How Do I Properly Spiritually Cleanse My Things/Place?

Let's start with the cleansing of individual items. If you have something that seems to be somehow haunted or have negative energy attached to it and you choose not to dispose of the item, there are things you can do. If you do decide to dispose of the piece, there are a few better ways to do it.

If possible, pour some salt on the item or douse it with salt

water or Florida Water or Holy Water and wrap it in newspaper. Then, if possible, take it somewhere remote and bury it – not on your own or anybody's private property! If this is not a viable option, take the item to a dump or public trash can or dumpster. If you can't wrap it, do what you can to break it. You don't want it to look appealing to someone who searches garbage for furniture and other things they can overhaul and then keep in their own home or sell. You do not want anyone else dealing with the problems you had.

A note about salt water. When I speak of salt water in terms of use in cleansing or blessing rituals I do not mean that even if you live in the middle of a landlocked area you must make a pilgrimage to the closest ocean and collect a few quarts or more of natural salt water. For these purposes, home made salt water is often most effective. To make salt water for ritual purposes you can use tap water (I was taught and strongly suggest boiling it to purify it). Distilled water or purified water boiled or not, is also fine. Let's say you are making a cup of salt water. Use one cup of the boiled (let it boil at least five minutes) water, or one cup of distilled or filtered water. You can also boil these, that is a matter of personal preference. Yes, you can also use Holy Water, in that case I would suggest not boiling it. It has already been through a cleansing process through the ritual the priest has already performed.

Another thing I would like to point out is that one often hears stories of people deciding to "test" to see if family members, friends or loved ones are oppressed or possessed by evil Christian beings and they put Holy Water into the person's drink. The

thinking is that if the person has no reaction, they are not being overtaken. If they do, this is the sign of the devil or a demon inside the person. While in concept this is fine and ideally would work, the reality is that it is potentially very dangerous. Most people procure their Holy Water from the front at their local church. It is very common to see people bring a bottle from home, submerge it in the bowl and then when the bottle is appropriately full, they cap it and walk away. This is the same water dozens of other people put their fingers in when blessing themselves and their spouses, children, etc. Even the cleanest infant or toddler can have all kinds of bacteria on their skin. The same is true of adults. Everyone may appear healthy, but everyone has bacteria on their skin. Also consider it is frequently when people are feeling sick that they stop into the church to anoint themselves with the water.

What this all comes down to is that Holy Water is usually, in a practical sense, filthy. It has bacteria from many hands, viruses, fecal matter (most people have a sick person around, a pet after which they clean up, steering wheels they touch after touching all kinds of things and more). This means that giving someone Holy Water in their iced tea could make them terribly sick. Various flu and cold germs are easily contracted and can be extremely dangerous to certain groups. Salmonella, e-coli, staff infections are all very serious and potentially lethal to people of all ages, even those in excellent health. Please, we are past the time of testing to see if people accused of Witchcraft float or not, let's not have you inadvertently responsible for someone becoming horrifically ill or worse, because you thought of slipping someone Holy Water in a drink. By the way, hot drinks will not necessarily

kill any germs that might be in public Holy Water. Just avoid this practice.

Say a prayer over the piece and burn it, outdoors. A good prayer would be one to Saint Benedict or Saint Michael, The Arch Angel or The Virgin Mother or Jesus. Keep in mind there are times when burning something is not ideal. It depends on WHAT the piece is. Ouija boards are a prime example here. The theory behind this is that if a Ouija board does indeed open a doorway to the other side, burning it may leave that doorway essentially uncloseable. This means the same problems could potentially be free to cause problems indefinitely. Worse, now that the door has been opened and cannot easily be shut and sealed, the "word" is out and any number of undesirable energies will find it and come through. There are some people who insist that burning a Ouija board worked extremely well for them. I will not argue if someone has personally had a positive outcome with something. Nevertheless, as a rule burning a Ouija board is not a great way to go. Other items of furniture, art or clothing can usually have their negative energy be dispersed by fire. Once more, pouring Holy Water, Florida Water or salt water on the item and into the ashes once it's burned can help make the burning rite as successful as possible. If you are uncertain what the best manner of disposal for am item might be, ask a local occult shop, clergy, etc.

Sage. Yes, here you go. When you are talking about a table, chair, piece of jewelry – anything which you can get under and around – you can light up your sage smudge stick and go to town waving the smoke all over the item. If it is something with doors or drawers, make sure they are all open and the smoke gets into

every part of the piece. This is very important and often people neglect to do it, thus allowing any unwanted entity to hide inside the drawers or doors until the smudge is over. While smudging you want to tell the entity it has to get out of the item and out of the house as well. Make sure you have a few windows cracked at least, if not wide open and if possible, while smudging the piece, move it near a door you can have open. There are two schools of thought here of which I am aware. The first says the furniture or whatever should be kept in the house and the windows and doors near it be open as much as possible for the energy to have a place to go.

A second theory says, take the item outside and smudge it there. That's not always possible depending on the size of whatever you are trying to clear of bad energies. There is a caveat to this though which is that many believe a cagey negative being (and let's face it, they are rarely stupid) can stay behind and climb right back into its happy place once it is returned inside.

My own teaching and experience is that keeping the item in has a better chance of sending the energy out.

Let's talk about sage for a moment. Sage is an herb used by many tribes of Native Americans throughout the Americas from Canada through the United States and into Mexico. In some traditions the sage is loose and burned in an abalone shell. The smoke is waved through the air by a Shaman, leader of various Earth based religions such as Wicca or Witchcraft (which though connected are not the same practice, but that could be a whole other book) or a lay person who has learned how to do it, using a feather. Traditionally, this would be an eagle feather, however,

those are no longer legal to have unless you are a card carrying member of a Native American tribe. Sometimes, additional paperwork is required if you want to carry one from one state to another or on an airplane. So, you can use a large bird feather (for example, a Turkey feather or something similar and not loose pieces of feather such as a peacock would have).

The act of moving the burning sage and wafting it through the air is known as "Smudging." There are also sticks of sage bound by cotton twine, known as "smudge sticks." They resemble big fat green cigars and are easier for most people to handle than the loose sage in the shell with the feather. There are also many kinds of sage. There is regular sage, used most in cooking. There is white sage which has a bit more bitter scent and larger leaves. Some people are not as fond of the scent of white sage, still, it is enormously popular. There is also clary sage which is something of a cross in scent between traditional and white sage. Many forms of sage which are sold for the purpose of smudging will also offer a mixture of the various stages as well as possibly sweet grass and lavender. Sweet grass can also be used for smudging purposes on its own as can rosemary. Another item that can be used to smudge away negativity is tobacco. Preferably not regular cigarettes, but pure tobacco burned in a shell or bundle as sage would be.

While sage has become an especially popular herb to use for cleansing the spirit or physical things since the 1980s, there are numerous herbs which can also be used. In our shop, if we have run out of sage, we have had people get so distressed they virtually go into spasms. There is no reason for this as so many other herbs can be used for the same purpose and are every bit as

potent or powerful. Some need to be burned on temple charcoal (fast lighting charcoal used to burn incense in most churches) and a metal container such as a censor or small cauldron. This is important because the charcoal burns very hot and will likely break a glass, ceramic or crockery burner.

With this in mind, here is a list of some wonderful herbs, resins and botanicals one can use to banish negativity around an individual item, on property or in a space. These can be purchased in their original forms and burned on charcoal or they can be found in stick incense form and burned that way. Despite claims about loose herbs being somehow more potent, stick incense is just as potent. Use what smells right to you and what you think will be more comfortable for you to use. Keeping the charcoal lit and continually dropping pinches of herbs into the container can be a little much for some people. If you are more comfortable with this way of doing things, that's great. In that case, know these negative/malevolent entity removing herbs and resins. Please also know to consult your local occult shop or trusted on-line dealer if there is no occult shop near you, about the loose incenses they carry for the purpose. Many will be proprietary blends. There should be a few for the same purpose to choose from in order that you like the scent. The issue here being that if you don't like the scent you will be less likely to use the product and then far less cleansing gets accomplished.

Here are some of the most common, tried and true, effective herbs, botanicals and resins to know about for the purpose of removing negative or evil energy:

- Sage
- White Sage
- Clary Sage
- Rosemary
- Holly
- Sweet Grass
- Cedar
- Sandalwood
- Pine
- Frankincense
- Myrrh
- Copal
- Palo Santo
- Rue
- Asafatida
- Sulfur (Though most people do not like it)
- Cayenne Pepper (If you intend to burn it, make sure the area is well ventilated)
- Storax (Gum Arabic)

These are all very powerful substances that have been used by different cultures all over the world for ages. These are all ingredients with various attributes, one specifically being the ability to help remove unwanted presences from things or places. They can be used alone, sometimes used in mixtures. Some you will find in stick incense form easily, some you will not. If you are going to use a stick incense, find the best quality you can. Many stick incenses, in particular ones made overseas, are made with a

base of ox or cow dung. That means they are less expensive, burn faster and masking the dung scent is more difficult, so they will have a heavier, more thickly perfumey scent. That's fine for some people, some find it quite bothersome. Stick incense made in The United States or Canada, for example, are generally wood based (a byproduct of the lumber industry) and burn slower. They also have no unpleasant base scent to cover so the oils used to scent them are as a rule, higher quality. This means they will usually be more expensive.

The things to consider here are whether you like it and that your intention plays a major role in successfully removing an energy that doesn't want to be removed. Most occultists, for example, do not use Asian/Indian Nag Champa incense. Most don't care for it and it is generally used for keeping a positive vibration in the home and not getting tough with (naturally clearing out) malevolence. However, if it is something you love and feel keeps you protected, feel free to try using it. The worst that is likely to happen is that it is ineffective. The spirits may let you know they didn't appreciate the attempted eviction, but the point is if you have a scent of incense you love and that makes you feel better when you're feeling low, it is important to take that into consideration.

If you are trying to cleanse a small item, such as a piece of jewelry, trinket box or other small sort of thing another way to cleanse it easily and effectively is to say a prayer over it for banishing negative or evil energies. Then place it in a plastic bag with a zipper closure along with some salt (as long as salt will not damage the finish or otherwise mar the piece) seal the bag and put

it in the freezer for a minimum of twenty-four hours. I personally have used this technique on numerous occasions and have had great success with it. My theory as to the reason this is powerful is that salt is one of the only materials known universally to be painful to spirits. Sealed up with the uncomfortable salt in the icy environment, something seems to happen that causes spirits to decide it isn't worth hanging on to whatever thing to which they've attached themselves. Plus, humans rarely spend much time inside their freezer, so human emotional reactions (which negative entities thrive on) are few. I am not sure if they jump through the freezer and leave, but it's a good reason to leave a door or window obviously open so they can get out. Or, perhaps when the bag is finally retrieved and opened their energy is so depleted it is not worth risking more of this treatment and they then leave

Either way, they do seem to leave. That's the important thing.

A Few Words About Salt

Virtually every culture that has ever recognized the existence of spirits has also discovered that salt is apparently painful to them. There many possible reasons for this. Salt can extract impurities from people, swimming pools, the air and so on. It stings when it touches open wounds or gets into one's eyes. So, there may be something about the removal of impurities or something about the chemical structure, we don't yet know for certain why, but we know human ghosts and spirits which may never have been human all seem to react strongly to salt.

There are many kinds of salt. The one which seems to have the most potency against spirits is Black Salt. This makes sense as not only is black a color of protection in many traditions, but this particular salt is probably grain for grain the most salty of all. It doesn't fully dissolve, so it is not ideal for ingesting. It does mean a grain can stay in a place and remain potent for some time. It is relatively simple to get black salt, most botanicas and Occult supply shops carry it. It is also not very expensive. Black Salt is my personal favorite salt to use for removing anything negative.

There is Sea Salt which is excellent for cooking and spiritual cleansing baths or rituals. It comes in fine to coarse grain and can vary in price. While more expensive than plain table salt, it is not pricey. Sea Salt is my second favorite salt for use to cleanse spirits.

Table Salt is the most common form of salt and is inexpensive and easy to find. Virtually anyone has it in their kitchen. This salt is always appropriate to use for any work to remove negative energies from a place. It's not as fancy and not as salty to taste. It is possible that those things make some difference to some extent in terms of efficacy in ritual to remove negative entities. However, this salt has been used for centuries with great success.

Epsom Salt is also a remover of negativity. Despite the name, it's really a magnesium, not a salt. It is great for detoxification baths and many use it as a laxative (again it is associated with purging the living body of toxins) and is also inexpensive. It has a bitter taste and thus is not used for cooking. Personally, I would not use it for purposes of removing spirits from a space.

For the purpose of removing anything negative from a space,

I prefer one of the first three salts mentioned here. However, some people do use Epsom Salt for this purpose and insist they have great results. There is much to be said for the power of faith and belief in the tools we use when dealing with ridding It is my belief that all these salts will be powerful for the purpose of spirit cleansing/removal. The most important matter may be one's reasons for using and feeling confident about a particular salt.

Simple, Highly Effective House Blessing and Cleansing Techniques

Smudging

Smudging is a simple technique which uses smoke from burning a product such as sage to cleanse a space. The reason something is burned is two fold. One, virtually every spirituality in the world believes smoke carries prayers to the God energy (however you see it) and gets the attention of that energy. Two, the herb, botanical, etc. being burned is in itself both an offering to the divine energy and has attributes of cleansing and purification in its own right. There are various ways to do this, but I have found this to be most effective. Start burning whatever you have decided to use as the smudge. I believe it is best to start in the very middle of the space and work your way to the outside. In some cases, it may be better to walk straight from the front to the back or back to the front of a building. This depends on the design of the place. The intention is to push anything negative out from the heart of the space to the outside. It is best to have all cabinets, drawers and closets slightly open so the smoke may

get into those places. Leave doors between rooms open. Go from the area farthest from the outside to the outside. Wave the smoke through each room. Some people like to use a smudging feather (associated with Native American spiritualities) to wave the smoke around. A hand fan, a hand or blowing the smoke around will do just as well.

Don't get too caught up in the tools. Use a smudge product you like. It can be sage, palo santo, an incense for house blessing. It can be loose incense burned on charcoal or stick incense. It's best if you like the scent. You don't want the lingering scent of something you find unpleasant. That will only remind you of the cleansing and possibly irritate you. Those feelings, no matter how minimal, can defeat the purpose of this ritual. You have to feel good about what you are doing. As you walk through the rooms, wave the smoke to the doors leading outside. Say a prayer, chant or affirmation that you like for the purpose. You can find these all over, write your own, whatever works for you. Something along the lines of "Only Love, Light and Peace may dwell in this home. All else does not belong." You would say it over and over while you walk through the space. It need not rhyme. People ask about these details frequently, so I am trying to cover all common questions. Work your way to the front door and outside. If you live in an apartment, smudge the front door and back door if you have one. If you live in a house and can go around property with the smudge while saying your prayer, do so. This is not something you should rush. It may feel a little awkward or silly, but you have already felt that it needs to be done, why worry about that? Ultimately, you and anyone else in the space will be happier there

and that is the point.

Once you have smudged your space thoroughly, I would then bring in blessings and seal the negativity out. You've just worked hard to smudge the place, if you don't want to have to do this frequently, seal the space next. This step is often overlooked or even unknown to people. It is a reason so many cleansings do not feel entirely successful very long. Sealing a space is not complicated. Spray holy water, Florida water, in the middle of each room toward the corners of each room. Or, anoint the doors and windows from the inside with olive oil, holy water or any other oil you have found that suits the purpose. If you are uncertain, consult your local occult shop or botanica. They will probably have many options of smudge and sealing oil to choose from. Continue your chant until you have done each window and door. End at the front door (do other doors that lead outside first). When you are satisfied with your ritual, end by saying something like, "It Is So."

Salt/Holy Water Blessing

This works pretty much the same way as smudging. However, instead of burning something and using incense or herbs, you use a small bowl of either blessed water, holy water or salt water you have made. I do think it best to meditate or pray over the water as you make it. Stand in the middle of each room and dip your fingers into the water. As you say your prayer or affirmation out loud, flick the water toward each corner in the room. Some

people like to do this with a few splashes of water toward each corner, whatever you feel comfortable with is fine. Just as with the smudging, do this throughout the house until you wind up ultimately at the front door. Flick some of the water at the door. If possible, go around the house and do this outside. Again, I would recommend sealing the rooms in the same way as mentioned before. If you have used water to cleanse, use an oil to seal out the negativity.

Candles

Some people prefer to do the smudge ritual using a candle. Walk through each room and do the same as you would with an incense or water. However, instead of spreading smoke or sprinkling water, you have a burning candle that is held in the middle of each room while chant or prayer is said. White candles are the most traditional here. It is also best to say your prayer several times over in each room if you are using only a candle. Again, after you have done the inside and outside, I recommend sealing the space. A variation on this is to have several candles which you light and leave one in each room as you go. If you prefer to do this remember to keep an eye on the candles and let each burn at least an hour after the ceremony is over. I have used this method in some very troubled spaces with excellent results.

Conclusion

Whether you discover there really is any sort of problematic energy or entity/entities in your space or not, information on the subject of the paranormal is key. My ultimate goal in writing this book is to do several things. First, if you think your home is haunted or there is anything unexplainable taking place – it's possible there is. Do not be afraid to reach out to your local paranormal research group, occult shop or a place like a university paranormal investigation study group. Certain universities DO have such classes and if not, they have professors of anthropology, psychology and others who know more than you may think about paranormal matters. In religious studies there are often people with backgrounds in the occult.

Do not let anyone laugh at you or bully you into staying quiet and living in lonely misery thinking that is your only option. It is not. If you don't get assistance from the first authority you consult, go to another. You can order books on the paranormal easily and inexpensively online. Though if possible go to a local occult shop. They may or may not have a large selection of books on the subject, but they should know something about it. And whether you decide to attempt to rid yourself or your space of unwanted energies yourself or to call in professionals (and please call in professional help if you have the slightest sense you could be in over your head, doing a haphazard job will bring poor results and

possibly make things worse) what is most important is to know things are not hopeless. Also, don't allow any religious group to force its agenda on you if you are not comfortable with it. This usually comes from people with your best interests at heart, but what works for someone else may not be a desirable way of life for you. Ultimately, the thing I feel most important to walk away with here is to have faith, even when it feels unbearably difficult. It is my firm belief **Light and Love Always Prevail. Always.**

www.ingramcontent.com/pod-product-compliance
Lightning Source LLC
Chambersburg PA
CBHW022117090426
42743CB00008B/891